SPITFIRE

OSPREY
PUBLISHING

SPITFIRE

TONY HOLMES

First published in Great Britain in 2015 by Osprey Publishing,
PO Box 883, Oxford, OX1 9PL, UK
1385 Broadway, 5th Floor, New York, NY 10018, USA
E-mail: info@ospreypublishing.com

Osprey Publishing is part of Bloomsbury Publishing Plc

In the compilation of this volume we relied on the following Osprey titles: DUE 5, *Spitfire vs Bf 109: Battle of Britain* by Tony Holmes; DUE 60, *Spitfire V vs C.202 Folgore* by Donald Nijboer; ACE 5, *Late Mark Spitfire Aces 1942–45* by Dr Alfred Price; ACE 12, *Spitfire Mark I/II Aces 1939–41* by Dr Alfred Price; ACE 16, *Spitfire Mark V Aces 1941–45* by Dr Alfred Price; ACE 81, *Griffon Spitfire Aces* by Andrew Thomas; ACE 98, *Spitfire Aces of North Africa and Italy* by Andrew Thomas; ACE 122, *Spitfire Aces of Northwest Europe 1944–45* by Andrew Thomas; and *The Battle of Britain* by Kate Moore. Additional material by Paul Eden.

Every attempt has been made by the Publisher to secure the appropriate permissions for material reproduced in this book. If there has been any oversight we will be happy to rectify the situation and written submission should be made to the Publishers.

A CIP catalogue record for this book is available from the British Library.

Alfred Price has asserted his right under the Copyright, Designs and Patents Act, 1988, to be identified as one of the Authors of this Work.

ISBN: 978 1 4728 1279 7
eBook ISBN: 978 1 4728 1281 0
PDF ISBN: 978 1 4728 1280 3

Index by Zoe Ross
Typeset in Sabon
Originated by PDQ Media, Bungay, UK
Printed in China through World Print Ltd.

16 17 18 19 20   11 10 9 8 7 6 5 4 3 2

Imperial War Museum Collections

Many of the photos in this book come from the Imperial War Museum's huge collections which cover all aspects of conflict involving Britain and the Commonwealth since the start of the twentieth century. These rich resources are available online to search, browse and buy at www.iwmcollections.org.uk.
Imperial War Museum: www.iwm.org.uk

Artwork

Front and back cover images, images on pages 39, 48, 52, 62 and 81 by Jim Laurier (Osprey Publishing); page 41 Chris Thomas (Osprey Publishing); page 56 Chris Davey (Osprey Publishing); page 65 Mark Postlethwaite (Osprey Publishing); page 88 Gareth Hector (Osprey Publishing).

Osprey Publishing is supporting the Woodland Trust, the UK's leading woodland conservation charity, by funding the dedication of trees.

www.ospreypublishing.com

The following will help in converting measurements:	
1 mile = 1.6km	1 yard = 0.9m
1lb = 0.45kg	1ft = 0.3m
	1in = 25.4mm
	1 Imp gal = 1.2 US gal

CONTENTS

INTRODUCTION

The fame of the Supermarine Spitfire is undoubtedly helped by its looks. Designed by R. J. Mitchell, the Spitfire's slender fuselage, long nose, and large, elliptical wing suggested the supreme aerodynamics that it indeed delivered. Yet its aesthetics were matched by its capacity to fight, and it crucially placed Britain on an equal footing with the German, Italian, and Japanese air forces for the duration of World War II.

MITCHELL'S CREATION

On 13 September 1931, the Supermarine S.6B seaplane won the Schneider Trophy outright for Britain at an average speed of 340.08mph. Looking to introduce a fighter of similar performance, the Air Ministry issued a specification for a new interceptor, against which Supermarine issued Mitchell's disappointing Type 224. An ungainly monoplane with fixed undercarriage, the aircraft first flew in February 1934 and lost out to the Gloster SS.37 biplane, which became the Gladiator.

Inspired by his work on the S.6B, Mitchell set about designing a new fighter around the Rolls-Royce PV.12 engine. The Air Ministry was interested enough to draw up a new specification, F.37/34, for the aircraft, which first flew as the Type 300 on 5 March 1936; it was soon named Spitfire. Tragically, given the Spitfire's subsequent history, Mitchell died the following year, but the Spitfire was developed further and entered RAF service in 1938.

OPPOSITE Three Spitfires of No. 19 Squadron grace the skies in 1939 shortly before the outbreak of war. (IWM CH 20)

A year later, Britain was at war and the Spitfire began its journey to becoming an aviation legend. Spitfires first fired their guns in anger on 6 September 1939, three days after Great Britain declared war on Germany. In fact, a technical malfunction at a radar station had caused British anti-aircraft batteries to open up on RAF aircraft, with 74 Squadron's Spitfires subsequently engaging 56 Squadron's Hurricanes in a short-lived encounter that cost two Hurricanes shot down.

Combat proper was entered on 16 October and many myths subsequently accrued around the Spitfire's role in the early war years, particularly in relation to the Battle of Britain, fought in the summer of 1940. For example, the lion's share of Britain's fighter response in fact went to the more numerous but slower and less agile Hurricanes; at the beginning of the battle, there were 27 squadrons of Hurricanes and 19 squadrons of Spitfires. The Hurricane also provided a more stable gunnery platform. Yet what the Spitfire gave the RAF was a combat aircraft that was able to take on the German Messerschmitt Bf 109E fighters on equal terms.

The Messerschmitt may have had a slightly faster top speed, particularly at high altitudes, and a better climb rate, but in practical combat conditions the Spitfire displayed a higher rate of turn, for a smaller turning circle, which allowed a good pilot to close down into a firing position if his German opponent allowed a turning fight to develop.

Of course, Germany improved its aircraft – both the Bf 109F and the Focke-Wulf Fw 190 outperformed the Spitfire when they initially appeared on the scene – hence the Spitfire itself was developed through numerous variants during the war. Wing and armament configurations changed, with 20mm cannon introduced, while the fighter-bomber versions could carry bombs. The Merlin was upgraded to keep

OPPOSITE As the war drew to a close, late mark Spitfires were used throughout Germany on armed reconnaissance missions, such as this Spitfire XVI belonging to No. 416 Squadron. (Canadian Forces)

pace with airframe development and the later marks employed the more powerful Rolls-Royce Griffon engine. Through engine, airframe and wing modifications different marks, even subvariants of marks, were optimised for fighting in different ways at particular altitudes. For example, a late-war variant, the Mk XIV fighter, had a top speed of 439mph, as much as 86mph faster than a fully equipped late-production Mk I.

The Fleet Air Arm (FAA) also had its own version, known as the Seafire.

Meanwhile, the Spitfire was sold to the air forces of other nations, for example, more than 1,000 Spitfires were provided to the Soviet Union, although the type proved somewhat fragile under that country's harsh operating conditions.

In total during the war years, 20,351 Spitfires were produced. They saw action across all theatres of the conflict, flown by the pilots of many nations – Americans, Australians, Canadians, Czechs, Indians, Poles, New Zealanders and South Africans, among others. The aircraft was the making of numerous aces, including the famous No. 74 Squadron pilot Adolph 'Sailor' Malan, whose final tally in Spitfires was 27 individual kills, seven shared kills, two unconfirmed, three probables and 16 damaged.

The excellence of the Spitfire design meant that the aircraft soldiered on around the world for at least a decade after the end of World War II, seeing combat in conflicts such as the 1947 Indo-Pakistan War and the 1948 Arab–Israeli War, while the final RAF combat sortie was flown by a PR.Mk 19 during the Malayan Emergency in 1954. Today, many examples remain airworthy, with more being restored all the time, such is the aircraft's continued popularity – even in the age of hyper-sophisticated jet fighters, there is something instantly appreciable, elegant, and powerful about the Spitfire.

OPPOSITE Seafire IIIs aboard an aircraft carrier. (Courtesy of Donald Nijboer)

CHRONOLOGY

1934

Feb R. J. Mitchell's first fighter design, the Vickers-Supermarine Type 224, powered by a Rolls-Royce Goshawk, makes its maiden flight.

1 Dec The British Air Ministry issues a contract to Vickers-Supermarine for the new Mitchell-designed, Rolls-Royce PV.12-powered monoplane fighter, writing Specification F.37/34 around it; it would evolve into the Spitfire.

OPPOSITE The Spitfire's ancestry can be traced directly to the Supermarine S 6B Schneider Trophy winner of 1931. This particular example, powered by a Rolls-Royce R engine, broke the world air speed record on 29 September 1931 when Flight Lieutenant George Stainforth reached 407.5 mph whilst at the controls. (Crown Copyright)

1936

5 Mar F.37/34 prototype Type 300 K5054 (later christened 'Spitfire'), powered by a Rolls-Royce Merlin C driving a two-bladed fixed pitch de Havilland propeller, makes its maiden flight from Eastleigh airfield, near Southampton.

June Vickers-Supermarine signs a contract with the Air Ministry to produce 310 Spitfire I aircraft.

1938

14 May First production Spitfire I makes its maiden flight one year later than planned due to a shortage of skilled labour and manufacturing difficulties.

4 Aug No. 19 Squadron at Duxford, Cambridgeshire becomes the first unit in RAF Fighter Command to be issued with the new Spitfire I.

1939

Sept First flight of the Mk II Spitfire.

16 Oct No. 603 Squadron shoots down a Ju 88 bomber over the Firth of Forth for the Spitfire I's first victory.

1940

Mar Merlin XX-engined Mk III undergoes trials.

23 May Spitfire Is and Bf 109Es clash for the first time when Nos 54 and 74 Squadrons tangle with I./JG 27 near the Dunkirk evacuation beaches.

June Production of the Spitfire II at the Nuffield factory in Castle Bromwich commences, with the first examples reaching No. 611 Squadron in July.

June Hispano 20mm cannon-armed Spitfire IB enters service with No. 19 Squadron.

Jul First Mk IIs delivered to the RAF.

10 Jul Battle of Britain officially commences, with 348 Spitfire Is, split between 19 Fighter Command squadrons, opposing eight Jagdgeschwader (fighter wings) equipped with 809 Bf 109Es.

13 Aug *Adlertag* (Eagle Day): Luftwaffe launches all-out offensive against the RAF but loses 45 aeroplanes to the RAF's 13.

31 Oct Battle of Britain officially ends, with Spitfire units having downed 521 German aircraft and Fighter Command having lost 403 Spitfires in combat. Some 610 Bf 109Es had been destroyed in action between 10 July and 31 October.

Dec Spitfire V prototype (K9788), powered by a Merlin 45 engine developing 1,470hp, makes its maiden flight.

1941

Jan First trials of the Spitfire Mk V; these were so successful that the Mk III was dropped and the Mk V rushed into production.

10 Jan First official *Circus* offensive mission into Europe includes three squadrons of Spitfires.

Spring Spitfire IIA (Long Range) fighters, equipped with 40Imp gal fixed fuel tank under port wing, commence operations over France.

June Six RAF fighter squadrons are fully equipped or in the process of converting to the Spitfire V.

5 Jul First flight of the pressurised, high-altitude Spitfire Mk VI.

27 Nov Maiden flight of the Griffon-engined Spitfire Mk IV.

1942

10 Jan Royal Navy Fighter School's commanding officer, Lieutenant Commander H. P. Bramwell, lands a modified Spitfire aboard the carrier HMS *Illustrious* in the River Clyde, the first step in development of the Seafire.

7 Mar 15 Spitfire Vs fly to Malta from the aircraft carrier HMS *Eagle*. By May five squadrons on Malta were equipped with the Mk V.

8 May Sergeant Wilbert Dodd of No. 185 Squadron, flying a Spitfire V from Malta, makes the first claim against the Macchi C.202, for one aircraft 'probably destroyed'.

June Last Spitfire IIs in Fighter Command retired by No. 152 Squadron. First Mk IXs delivered.

Summer Spitfires battle Italian C.202s for Malta; the Luftwaffe concedes defeat on 11 October.

Aug	First pressurised, high-altitude Spitfire Mk VII leaves the Supermarine production line.
8 Aug	Spitfire Mk 20, the second Griffon-engined Spitfire, flies for the first time.
Nov	First production Spitfire Mk VIII and PR.Mk XI built.
Dec	Second Spitfire Mk 20 redesignated as Spitfire Mk 21. Seafire Mk 45 later produced as navalised version.

1943

	Use of Spitfire as a fighter-bomber gains momentum after trials at unit level over North Africa in 1942.
Feb	No. 41 Squadron begins conversion onto the Griffon-engined Spitfire Mk XII.
Mar	Spitfire PR.Mk XIII tested at Boscombe Down.
Summer	Mk VIII JF299 becomes the first Spitfire modified with a 'cut-down' rear fuselage and 'teardrop' canopy.
27 Nov	The first Seafire F.Mk III carrier fighters reach 894 Naval Air Squadron (NAS).

1944

Jan	No. 610 Squadron begins receiving the Spitfire Mk XIV.
Feb	Griffon-engined Seafire XV flies for the first time.
May	High-altitude, pressurised Spitfire PR.Mk X and Griffon-engined Spitfire PR.Mk XIX enter service.
6 June	D-Day; Spitfires provide fighter cover over the landing beaches, and in the following months help push the Germans back to extend the beachhead and allow for the Allied breakout.

OPPOSITE Spitfires of No. 610 Squadron flying over the Channel in 'vic' formation on 24 July 1940, during the early stages of the Battle of Britain. (IWM CH 740)

ABOVE A preserved PR Mk XI Spitfire at Royal International Air Tattoo, Fairford, Gloucestershire, in 2008. (Adrian Pingstone)

Summer	Spitfires used against V-1 flying bombs that the Germans begin launching at London.	
19 Aug	Battle for Normandy over; German forces withdraw while Allied armies and air forces follow closely on their heels.	
Sept	Production of the Packard Merlin-engined Spitfire MK XVI begins.	

1945

1 April	Flying a Seafire, Lieutenant R. H. Reynolds shoots down two Japanese Mitsubishi A6M5 Zero fighters; these are the first Seafire victories against the type.
Mar	First Spitfire Mk 22 delivered. Seafire Mk 46 later produced as navalised variant.
June	Spitfire Mk 18 flies for the first time.

| 15 Aug | In one of the last dogfights of World War II, a mixed formation of eight Seafire L.Mk IIIs and F.Mk IIIs encounters four Imperial Japanese Navy Mitsubishi J2M3 Raidens and eight A6M5c and A6M7 Zero-sens over Tokyo Bay. The result is seven Zero-sens shot down for the loss of one Seafire. |
| Nov | Seafire Mk XVII enters service. |

1946

| April | Production of Spitfire Mk 24 begins. Seafire Mk 47 produced as navalised version. |

1948

| Jan | Seafire Mk 47 enters service. |
| Feb | The last Spitfire, a Mk 24, comes off the production line. Seafire Mk 45 withdrawn. |

1949

| Oct | No. 800 Naval Air Squadron (NAS) begins rocket attacks in Malaya. Operations continue until February 1950. |

1950

| June | No. 800 NAS sails for Korea, flying 360 combat sorties during the conflict. |
| Aug | Seafire Mk 46 withdrawn. |

1952

| Jan | No. 80 Squadron retires the RAF's last frontline fighter Spitfires – Mk 24s. |

1954

| 1 April | A Spitfire PR.Mk 19 flies the type's last operational RAF sortie. |
| 23 Nov | No. 764 NAS retires the FAA's last operational Seafires, all of them Mk XVIIs. |

DESIGN AND DEVELOPMENT

Vickers-Supermarine, the manufacturer of one of history's greatest aircraft, in fact had little experience of building fighter aircraft prior to placing the Spitfire into production. Its predecessor Supermarine had, however, been heavily involved in high-performance aviation through its family of flying-boat and floatplane racers of the 1920s and early 1930s.

Based in Woolston, Southampton, the company, and its chief designer, Reginald J. Mitchell, initially achieved prominence internationally when Supermarine's Sea Lion biplane won the Schneider Trophy competition for seaplanes in 1922. Over the next nine years the company would secure further racing successes, and set world speed records, with its S.4, S.5, S.6 and S.6B floatplanes. A fruitful relationship with Rolls-Royce's aeroengine division was also cultivated during this period.

OPPOSITE The Rolls-Royce V-shaped, inline 12-cylinder Merlin engine. (IWM ATP 10397G)

Vickers Aviation had acquired a majority shareholding in Supermarine in 1928, and this helped the company survive the lean inter-war period when few military orders were on offer. Indeed, the bulk of Supermarine's work during this time centred on the construction of 79 Southampton flying-boats for the RAF.

THE EARLY YEARS

In 1931 the Air Ministry issued Specification F.7/30 for a new fighter for frontline service with the RAF that would boast a higher top speed than the 225mph Bristol Bulldog – little more than half the speed of the S.6B

Schneider Trophy winner! The winning design would also have to be armed with four .303in machine guns, which was double the armament of the RAF's biplane fighters then in squadron service.

Because military orders were scarce for the British aviation industry at the time the F.7/30 specification was issued, no fewer than eight manufacturers produced prototypes in response. Supermarine's 660hp Rolls-Royce Goshawk-powered Type 224 was one of three monoplane prototypes put forward. The Goshawk engine used the newly developed evaporative-cooling system rather than conventional external radiators, which meant that it could feature cleaner aerodynamics. The Type 224, with its distinctive low-mounted gull wing and fixed trousered undercarriage, made its first flight in February 1934, and the combination of evaporative cooling and the low-wing monoplane design soon presented Supermarine with serious engine overheating problems.

The aircraft's performance was also disappointing, with a top speed of just 238mph due to its overly thick wing and fixed undercarriage. It came as no surprise, therefore, that Gloster's SS.37 biplane, which was marginally faster and considerably more manoeuvrable, was chosen as the winner. Developed from the company's successful Gauntlet, the new fighter would enter service with the RAF as the Gladiator – Britain's last biplane fighter.

Undaunted by this initial failure, Mitchell and his team started work on a far cleaner airframe that would feature a retractable undercarriage and a considerably more powerful engine. The latter had emerged from Rolls-Royce in late 1934 in the form of the PV.12 (later renamed the Merlin). The company rated the engine at 790hp when unveiled, but hoped to eventually get 1,000hp from it. By this time Mitchell was already seriously ill with cancer. In 1933 he had taken a holiday to Europe to convalesce from an operation, and had met with some German aviators. He became convinced that war was inevitable and was determined to make his contribution by providing the design for a battle-winning fighter.

At the same time Vickers allocated funds for Mitchell and his team to proceed with their PV.12-powered fighter, which was designated Supermarine Type 300. Although begun as a private venture at Woolston, the Air Ministry quickly became interested in the aircraft. On 1 December 1934 it issued a contract worth £10,000 to Supermarine for construction of a prototype to Mitchell's 'improved F.7/30' design, under a new specification designated F.37/34.

The new Rolls-Royce engine was a third larger, both in terms of its weight and size in comparison with the Goshawk, so in order to compensate for the forward shift in the centre of gravity the sweepback of the leading edge of the fighter's wing was reduced. Soon, the wing had taken on an elliptical shape, as aerodynamicists at Supermarine calculated that this would create the lowest induced drag in flight. Such a flying surface also meant that the wing root would be thick enough to house the undercarriage when retracted.

Beverley Shenstone, the aerodynamicist on the Type 300 team, told noted aviation historian Dr Alfred Price:

I remember once discussing the shape with R. J. Mitchell, and he said jokingly 'I don't give a bugger whether it's elliptical or not, so long as it covers the guns!' The ellipse was simply the shape that allowed us the thinnest possible wing with sufficient room inside to carry the necessary structure and the things we wanted to cram in.

Mitchell's mentioning of the guns in this quote reflects the fact that in April 1935 Supermarine was asked by the Operational Requirements section of the Air Ministry to double the firepower being installed into the wings of its new fighter by fitting eight rather than four .303in Browning machine guns. Each gun would have its own 300-round ammunition box.

One of the final problems overcome with the prototype Type 300 prior to the aircraft being rolled out for the first time centred on the cooling for the PV.12 engine. Rolls-Royce had hoped to use the evaporative system once again, but this had performed so badly in the Type 224 that Mitchell was forced to go with an

external radiator, accepting the drag it produced. However, a newly developed ducted radiator designed by Fred Meredith of the Royal Aircraft Establishment (RAE) promised to offset the drag through its ability to expel compressed, heated air at increased velocity through a divergent duct. Thus, when the prototype F.37/34 was rolled out of the Woolston works on the banks of the River Itchen for the first time in February 1936, it boasted a Meredith-type ducted radiator beneath its starboard wing.

Following a series of ground runs, the fighter was dismantled and trucked to Supermarine's airfield at nearby Eastleigh. Once reassembled and passed fit to fly by the Aeronautical Inspection Directorate, the unpainted Type 300, wearing the serial K5054 and RAF roundels, took to the skies at 4.30pm. At the controls was Vickers' chief test pilot, Captain Joseph 'Mutt' Summers, who was aloft for just eight minutes.

OPPOSITE The Spitfire prototype, K5054, which flew for the first time on 6 May 1936. It would be a full 26 months before the first production Spitfire would have its maiden flight. (IWM MH 5214)

By early April the initial test programme had been completed, and on 26 May the prototype was delivered to the RAF trials establishment at Martlesham Heath. After a brief series of early flights had revealed the fighter's potential (including a top speed of 349mph), the Air Ministry signed a contract with Vickers-Supermarine for 310 fighters. There was some debate over what the new fighter should be called. According to the historian Robert Bungay, Vickers appeared to think of aeroplanes as 'bad tempered women'. They had previously come up with 'Shrew', but Mitchell apparently objected to this denigration of his elegant design. The eventual name actually came from the Vickers Chairman, Sir Robert Maclean, who called his daughter 'a little Spitfire', and it was approved by the Air Ministry.

As the sole prototype, K5054 was progressively modified into a more representative frontline fighter. For example, in August 1936 the aircraft returned to Eastleigh for the installation of eight machine guns, a reflector gunsight and radio. Ever more powerful versions of the Merlin engine were also fitted during 1936 and 1937.

On 11 June 1937, with K5054 still the only airworthy Spitfire in existence, its creator, Reginald J. Mitchell, succumbed to cancer aged just 42, having dedicated his health and the final years of his life to creating the aeroplane. In the wake of his death, Supermarine's chief draughtsman Joe Smith was promoted to chief designer, and he took charge of the Spitfire's development.

One of the more persistent problems facing Smith and his team was freezing of the wing guns, a problem first identified during a climb to 32,000ft for high-altitude firing trials during early 1937. This issue first arose in March 1937, and it was not effectively cured until October the following year – the ducting of hot air from the underwing radiator eventually solving the problem. By then the first production aircraft had at last reached Fighter Command, some 12 months later than scheduled.

The stressed-skin structure of the hand-finished prototype had proven difficult to replicate when it came to building production aircraft in jigs. The aircraft's elliptical wings could not be built using existing production techniques, and, being all metal, they were difficult to make and repair. Progress to this point had also been slowed by redrafting of the prototype drawings so that they could be used as blueprints from which to build combat-capable Spitfires – this took a year to complete. Once it came time to cut, forge or cast metal, Supermarine encountered further problems employing sufficiently skilled workers to man its production line.

Mitchell had sacrificed everything for performance, and as a result, a Spitfire took two-and-a-half times as long to build as a Hurricane and twice as long as a Bf 109E. With its 500-strong workforce fully occupied producing fuselages, Supermarine had to sub-contract work on the wings out to General Aircraft and Pobjoy; wing ribs to Westland; leading edges to The Pressed Steel Company; ailerons and elevators to Aero Engines Ltd; tails to Folland; wingtips to General Electric; and fuselage frames to J. Samuel White & Company. Final assembly and engine installation was completed at Eastleigh.

OPPOSITE The very first production Spitfire I built, K9787, made its maiden flight on 5 May 1938.

The Air Ministry was so dismayed by this convoluted process that in 1938 it contracted the Nuffield Organisation (which mass-produced cars) to build 1,000 Spitfire IIs in a new Shadow Factory at Castle Bromwich, and the first of these aircraft was delivered to the RAF in early July 1940. These Spitfires were also delayed by various factors: changes to the production specification by the Air Ministry, the factory management's ignorance about aerospace technology and squabbles between the unions and management over pay.

By then the production Spitfire I had matured into a frontline fighter to rival the best in the world. Among numerous changes made to the aircraft was the replacement of the original two-bladed, fixed-pitch Watts wooden propeller with a three-bladed two-pitch or variable-pitch de Havilland or Rotol airscrew. A bulged canopy had replaced the low, flat cockpit canopy, giving more headroom for taller pilots, while steel armour had been fitted behind and beneath the pilot's seat. A thick slab of laminated glass was also fitted to the front of the windscreen, and Identification Friend or Foe (IFF) transponders were built into the aircraft to identify it as friendly to the radar stations along the coast of Great Britain.

No. 19 Squadron became the first Fighter Command unit to receive Spitfire Is, in August 1938, and by September of the following year the RAF had ten squadrons equipped with the aircraft.

THE EARLY WAR YEARS

The Battle of Britain had proven the Spitfire I and II to be the right fighters at the right time. Designed as a pure interceptor, the Spitfire, when married with Britain's integrated radar air defence system, performed brilliantly. Indeed, without it the battle may have been lost. A veteran of the fighting with No. 54 Squadron

OPPOSITE The first RAF unit to receive Spitfire Is was No. 19 Squadron, which began replacing its Gauntlets with Supermarine fighters from August 1938. Based at RAF Duxford, the unit entertained the Fleet Street press for the first time on 4 May 1939, when this photograph was taken.

in 1940, New Zealand Spitfire ace Al Deere wrote:

> There can be no doubt that the Spitfire made victory in the Battle of Britain possible. Although there were more Hurricanes than Spitfires in the Battle, the Spitfire was the RAF's primary weapon because of its better all-round capability. The Hurricane alone could not have won this great air battle, but the Spitfire could have done so.

The numbers speak for themselves. Recent research and in-depth analysis by authors John Alcon and Dilip Sarkar reveal the Spitfire's true effectiveness during the Battle of Britain. The 30 squadrons of Hurricanes claimed 656 aircraft shot down, of which 222 were Bf 109s. The 19 squadrons of Spitfires, however, were credited with 529 Luftwaffe aircraft, of which no fewer than 282 were Bf 109s. As these figures show, the Spitfire was more than a match for the Luftwaffe's principal fighter type, hence the fact Fighter Command tasked units equipped with the Supermarine aircraft with engaging Bf 109s escorting German bombers, leaving the latter for the more numerous Hurricanes whenever possible.

At the beginning of the Battle of Britain the RAF was equipped with 19 squadrons of Spitfire Is. Production of the Mk I had commenced in April 1938 and it continued until March 1941, by which time 1,567 examples had been built. By June 1940 the Spitfire II had begun to appear. The new Mk II was powered by the Merlin XII, which produced 1,175hp. Top speed for the Mk II increased to 370mph, making the aircraft 15mph faster than the Spitfire I. Rate-of-climb was improved to the tune of 473ft a minute more than the Mk I. Furthermore, the new engine was fitted with a Coffman automatic starter, thus reducing the amount of time it took to get the aircraft off the ground. Deliveries of the first Spitfire IIs began in late August 1940, and by October, 195 had been delivered.

Contrary to many popular accounts, this is nowhere near the end of the story, however, since the Spitfire

OPPOSITE On 31 October 1938, six Spitfire Mk Is of No.19 Squadron take to the air. (IWM CH 21)

went through further developments, proving it to be one of the finest fighters of the war. However, its greatest attribute had nothing to do with its exceptional performance, but its capacity for continual development.

Ernest Hives, head of Rolls-Royce's aeroengine division, knew that the Merlin had yet to reach its full potential, which would in turn increase the performance of the Spitfire. Near the end of 1939 Hives began work on upgrading the Merlin II into the Merlin XX. Run on 100-octane fuel, as opposed to the 85-octane in operational use at that time, and fitted with a two-speed supercharger, the new engine produced 1,390hp – the Merlin II was rated at 1,030hp.

Supermarine was also refining the Spitfire airframe, cleaning up its lines and making it ready to accommodate the heavier engine. The fuselage was slightly lengthened, the undercarriage strengthened and the tailwheel made retractable. Impressed by the new variant, the Air Ministry ordered a prototype and designated it Mk III (serial N3297). Flown by Jeffrey Quill on 16 March 1940, the Spitfire III was judged 'satisfactory' in trials.

Incredibly, the Air Ministry was still unsure about the Spitfire's future. During a conference in early 1940 the subject of Fighter Command's future equipment with either the Spitfire III or new Hawker Typhoon was discussed, and the Air Ministry voiced a preference for the latter. The Battle of Britain, however, would solidify the Spitfire's reputation and future development. A strong advocate of the aeroplane was Lord Beaverbrook, Minister of Aircraft Production. With his advocacy, attitudes towards the Spitfire quickly changed, and in October 1940 1,000 Mk IIIs were ordered.

Parallel to this development was the creation of a new type of Rolls-Royce engine that was considerably more powerful than the Merlin. Known as the Griffon, it incorporated technology that had been used in the famous 'R' engines fitted to Mitchell's Schneider Trophy floatplanes. The Griffon was a big leap forward. Although slightly larger than the Merlin, it could still be mounted to the Spitfire airframe without the latter having to be significantly redesigned. Supermarine estimated that the new fighter would boast a top speed of 420mph. In May 1940 a formal contract was issued for the production of two prototypes, known as Mk IVs. In November 1941 the first prototype (DP845) took to the air, with impressive results.

Progress on the new Mks III and IV was slow, however. In the autumn of 1940 the Merlin XX engine was in short supply, the two-speed supercharger making it more complex to manufacture, while in an effort to keep the Hurricane competitive on the Channel front, the Air Ministry decided that the revised Mk II should receive the Merlin XX ahead of the Spitfire III. Then developments in Germany forced the RAF's hand when it came to acquiring a new Spitfire variant.

At the beginning of October 1940 three new Bf 109F-0 pre-production machines were delivered for service evaluation by the Luftwaffe on the Channel front. Compared to the Bf 109E, the new 'Friedrich'

featured a cleaner aerodynamic shape and more powerful engine. It had a top speed of 373mph at 19,700ft and a service ceiling of 36,100ft, making it clearly superior to the Spitfire II. Fighter Command reacted quickly. Air Vice-Marshal Sholto Douglas, head of Fighter Command, wrote an urgent letter to Lord Beaverbrook, stating:

I am concerned about the inferiority in the performance of our fighter aircraft compared with newer types of enemy fighters. The improved '109 not only out climbs our fighters from about 25,000ft but it is faster at altitude and has a better ceiling. This confers the tactical initiative on the enemy.

Critically, the Spitfire III (the variant originally intended to replace the Mks I and II) was not ready. Getting it into full production was also proving difficult, as converting existing production lines would involve considerable retooling and a great deal of time – something the RAF did not have. The Merlin XX, with its redesigned supercharger with separate blowers for high-altitude and low-altitude flying, was a complicated engine, and one Rolls-Royce could not build in sufficient numbers. Something had to be done, and quickly.

THE MK V

In October 1940 Rolls-Royce and Supermarine turned to the Merlin 45 (and later 46) engine. Developed in parallel with the Merlin XX by Rolls-Royce, it was effectively a simplified version of the new engine with the low altitude blower deleted. Developing 1,515hp with +16lb boost at 11,000ft, the new Merlin 45 was no larger than earlier variants of the engine, which meant that it could be easily fitted into existing Spitfire I/II airframes. The Merlin 45 was also easier to mass-produce than the Merlin XX. Rolls-Royce soon received instructions to re-engine 23 Spitfire Is, thus creating the first Mk Vs.

In January 1941 flight trials of the new fighter commenced, and these went so well that the more complex Mks III and IV were ultimately dropped and the Spitfire V rushed into production. Early-build Mk Vs were effectively Spitfire I and II airframes fitted with Merlin 45 engines. The heavier weight of the new engine and additional equipment added extra stress to the original Spitfire I airframes, however, which limited their operational capabilities. Production of the Spitfire VC from early October 1941 rectified these problems through the introduction of a significant number of improvements to the fighter.

During the Battle of Britain, Spitfire pilots had found that high-speed combat above 400mph caused the fighter's ailerons to lock up. A great deal of strength needed to be exerted in order to get any kind of movement out of the machine in the rolling plane. The problem was soon isolated – high-speed airflow over the fabric-covered ailerons caused them to balloon out, leaving them ineffective. The solution was a simple one – replace the fabric with a light alloy. Another problem that frustrated the young Spitfire pilots was the enemy's ability to simply dive out of trouble.

The Bf 109E's fuel injection system was superior to the Spitfire's float-type carburettor, which caused the engine to cut out during any negative-G manoeuvre. Anti-G modifications to the SU carburettor soon rectified the problem, and this 'fix' was subsequently fitted to the new Merlin 45/46 engine.

When the time came to send the notoriously short-ranged Spitfire to Malta, a two-part solution had to be found to the problem of getting the aircraft to the island. Early in 1940 Hurricanes had been successfully launched off an aircraft carrier and flown to Malta, but replicating this feat with a Spitfire V meant a 660-mile one-way flight, which was far in excess of the fighter's range. To address the problem, Supermarine developed a 90Imp gal jettisonable slipper tank. It proved successful, and subsequent Spitfire VBs and VCs were equipped with the necessary plumbing to accept the store. The new Spitfire V would also have to be

LEFT The clean and graceful lines of the Spitfire are clearly seen here as a Mk VB of No. 92 Squadron is banked for the photographer by its pilot. (Courtesy of Donald Nijboer)

tropicalised for the conditions on Malta, and later, in North Africa.

The fine dust it would encounter was an engine killer, for it entered the Merlin and caused excess wear, lower power output and a shortened lifespan. To battle the dust, the Vokes filter was added. Housed in a beard-like faring under the fighter's nose, the filter was very 'draggy' and unpopular with pilots. It reduced the Mk V's top speed, but its benefits far outweighed any reduction in performance caused by excessive wear. Other tropical items were also added. Fitted in the rear fuselage behind the cockpit was a tank for 1.5Imp gal of drinking water, along with a container of flying rations, an emergency tool roll, emergency equipment and a signal pistol with cartridges.

The Spitfire V also introduced the new C-type or 'Universal' wing. The original A-type wing design carried eight .303in Browning machine guns with 300 rounds per gun. The B-type was modified to carry two 20mm drum-fed Hispano Mk II cannons with 60 rounds per gun, plus four .303in Brownings. The C-wing was structurally modified to reduce the amount of effort required to rearm the weapons and to allow for the fitment of a combination of mixed armament – A-type, B-type or four 20mm cannon. The ammunition supply for the latter was doubled to 120 rounds per gun. The first Spitfire Vs were A-models armed with eight .303in Browning machine guns, followed by cannon-armed Mk VBs and VCs.

The Spitfire VC's wing was strengthened, and it introduced the new laminated windscreen design as seen on the Mk III. As with late-build Mk VBs, some Mk VCs were built with metal ailerons, while the main undercarriage legs were raked 2in further forwards to improve ground handling. Armour was increased to 193lb.

The rush to get the Spitfire V into service meant that some early machines suffered faults. According to Jeffrey Quill more than 20 Spitfires (mostly Mk VBs) were lost due to mainframe or engine failure. The airframe failures were traced to longitudinal instability. This was due largely to the shift in centre of gravity

ABOVE This VC Trop was photographed just after being loaded onto the aircraft carrier USS *Wasp*, as part of Operation *Calendar* in early April 1942. The fighter is equipped with a full armament of four 20mm cannon and eight .303in machine guns. Note the 'missing' wingtips crammed into the Spitfire's open cockpit. (Courtesy of Donald Nijboer)

towards the rear of the aircraft. New equipment, of course, meant more weight, and by 1943 a study carried out by the RAE at Farnborough showed that the average speed of a late production Mk V was slower than that of the original Mk I!

While Fighter Command redressed the balance with the 'stop gap' Spitfire V in early 1941, the Fleet Air Arm would also benefit from the development of this variant. Desperate for a single-engined carrier fighter with the performance to match the fabled Spitfire, the Admiralty demanded the creation of a navalised version. The first Spitfire to be 'hooked' was Mk VB BL676 in late 1941, and after encouraging carrier trials, 250 Mk VBs and VCs were earmarked for conversion. The new aircraft was named Seafire.

The Mk V would have the longest combat career of all the Spitfire variants to see action during World War II. Even after the Mk IX had superseded the Mk V as a high-altitude fighter, the older variant continued as a low-altitude machine. Fitted with a Merlin optimised for low-level work, the LF.Mk V

would equip 11 squadrons assigned to the Air Defence of Great Britain (ADGB) as late as June 1944.

Always a compromise, the Spitfire V was nevertheless again the right fighter at the right time. Its speed, armament and ceiling gave it the edge it needed in combat and a total of 6,472 Mk Vs was built – 94 Mk VAs by Supermarine, 3,911 Mk VBs (776 by Supermarine, 2,995 at Castle Bromwich and 140 by Westland) and 2,467 Mk VCs (478 by Supermarine, 1,494 by Castle Bromwich and 495 by Westland).

SPITFIRE MK IX, MK VII AND MK VIII

The Fw 190 first appeared over occupied France and the English Channel in September 1941. The new

OPPOSITE The first Spitfire VCs delivered to Malta were the most heavily armed Supermarine fighters of the war, featuring four Hispano Mk II 20mm cannon. Persistent stoppages due to faulty ammunition soon forced RAF armourers on Malta to remove two of the 20mm cannon, however. Spitfire armament on the island varied throughout the campaign, and it was not uncommon for aircraft to be fitted with just two 20mm cannon and two Browning .303in machine guns as seen here. (Osprey Publishing)

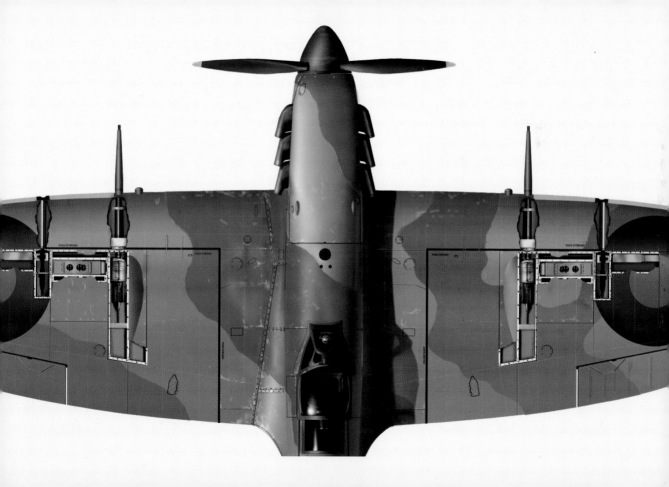

German fighter was greatly superior to the Mk V Spitfire that equipped most of Fighter Command's day fighter units – it was more than 20mph faster at all altitudes and it could out-climb, out-dive and out-roll the British fighter. Fighter Command's losses in offensive operations over occupied Europe rose alarmingly.

RAF fighter pilots were far from reticent about the qualities of their formidable new opponent. Their reports were relayed up the chain of command, gathering force as they did so, until they arrived on the desk of the Commander in Chief Fighter Command, Air Chief Marshal Sir Sholto Douglas. Adding his powerful voice to the clamour, Douglas wrote to the Ministry of Aircraft Production, demanding a fighter that could engage the Focke-Wulf from a position of equality or, preferably, superiority. The Ministry, in its turn, relayed his demand to the aircraft manufacturers.

One answer would have been to design and build a completely new fighter, but even on the most optimistic time scale it would have taken at least four years to bring it into service and Fighter Command could not afford to wait that long. Of the existing types, the Hawker Typhoon, then on the point of entering service, was as fast as the Fw 190 below 10,000ft, but suffering teething troubles, and above 20,000ft it was slower than the German fighter.

Fortunately for the RAF the solution to its most pressing problem was on the point of becoming a reality. Earlier in 1941, in response to a request to improve the high-altitude performance of the Merlin, Rolls-Royce engineers fitted a Merlin 45 with two supercharger blowers in series, one feeding into the other. Between the outlet of the first blower and the inlet of the second there was an extra cooling system – an intercooler – to reduce the temperature of the charge, and therefore increase its density.

The effect of the two-stage supercharger on the Merlin's high-altitude performance was striking. At 30,000ft the Merlin 45, with a normal single-stage supercharger developed about 720hp. At the same altitude, the same basic engine with the two-stage supercharger developed around 1,020hp.

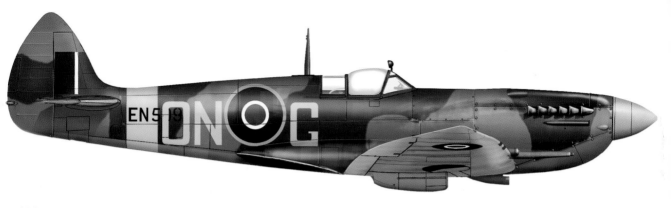

ABOVE Spitfire VII of Flight Lieutenant W. J. Hibbert, No. 124 Squadron, Bradwell Bay, 31 May 1944. Along with his squadronmates, during May Hibbert regularly patrolled the Thames Estuary, before then becoming part of the fighter escort for the D-Day landings and the days that followed. (Osprey Publishing)

The additional blower, the intercooler, and their respective casings added only about 200lb to the weight of the Merlin 45 and increased its length by just 9in. The Merlin with two-stage supercharging was designated Mark 60 and a revised version for installation in fighters was designated Mk 61.

In the summer of 1941, shortly before the Fw 190 appeared on the scene, Rolls-Royce engineers fitted a Merlin 61 into Spitfire N3297, a Mk III employed as an engine test bed. The intercooler required its own radiator so the aircraft was modified with two rectangular-section radiator housings of similar external shape, one under each wing. The port housing contained the oil cooler radiator and half of the main coolant radiator; the starboard housing contained the intercooler radiator and the other half of the main coolant radiator. To absorb the Merlin 61's extra power, the aircraft was fitted with a four-bladed propeller.

The unarmed, experimental Merlin 61 Spitfire made its first flight on 27 September 1941, just three weeks after the operational debut of the Fw 190. Initially there were problems with the intercooler, but by the end of the year the new engine was working satisfactorily. Early in 1942, N3297 went to the RAF test establishment at Boscombe Down for service trials, where it demonstrated a considerable improvement in performance compared with previous versions of the fighter: its maximum level speeds were recorded as 391mph at 15,900ft, 414 mph at 27,200ft and 354mph at 40,000ft. Rate of climb was much superior to that of the Spitfire Mk V, and the new Spitfire's service ceiling was estimated at 41,800ft.

The promise of greatly improved performance from the Merlin 61 also spawned the development of the Spitfire Mk VII and VIII. The former was a dedicated high-altitude fighter with a pressurised cabin. Based on the earlier Mk VI, it too was fitted with pointed wing tips that increased span by 3ft 4in and area by 6.5sq ft. To provide sufficient fuel for a high-speed climb to 40,000ft, perhaps followed by a lengthy tailchase, the internal fuel capacity of the Mk VII was raised to 124Imp gal – 40 per cent more than previous Merlin-engined Spitfire fighters. The airframe was redesigned and strengthened to enable it cope with the extra weight and, to reduce drag, the Mk VII was fitted with a retractable tailwheel.

The Mk VIII was essentially similar to the Mk VII, except that it did not have the pressurised cabin and usually employed the regular rounded wing tips. It offered an optimised combination of Merlin 61 and airframe, while the Spitfire Mk IX always required careful piloting since the more powerful engine could easily lead to overstressing of what was, essentially, a Mk V airframe. The task of redesigning the airframes of the Mks VII and VIII, and re-tooling the production lines to build them, took several months however, delaying their entry into service. Until they became available in quantity, the RAF's priority was therefore

ABOVE This late-war Spitfire IX belonged to No. 331 (Norwegian) Squadron, and on 29 January 1944 it was flown on a bomber escort mission by future ace Second Lieutenant Ragnar Dogger. (S. Heglund via Cato Guhnfeld)

the interim Mk IX, which proved so successful that it spawned the later Packard Merlin-engined Mk XVI. Between them, these two variants became the dominant Merlin Spitfire over Northwestern Europe in the later stages of the war, while the Mk VII was built in limited numbers and the majority of Mk VIIIs was delivered directly overseas.

GRIFFON SPITFIRES

In its development of a new aeroengine, Rolls-Royce began work on the Griffon shortly before the outbreak of war. With a cubic capacity one-third greater than that of the Merlin, the Griffon II with a single-stage supercharger developed 1,735hp. It was soon evident that the Spitfire could be modified to take the more powerful engine, and the first prototype of the Griffon-powered fighter, designated Mk IV, flew in November 1941. It was soon re-designated as the Mk XII and first flew operationally with No. 41 Squadron, which received the aircraft in April 1943. These Griffon-powered Spitfires were among the most impressive piston-engined fighters of their time; they could fly at 397mph at 18,000ft. While never produced in numbers comparable with their Merlin predecessors, they were a crucial development for the iconic aircraft as it countered low-altitude, high-speed Luftwaffe 'tip-and-run' fighter-bomber attacks along the English coast.

One hundred Mk XIIs were ordered by the RAF, essentially as Mk Vs with the minimum amount of modification necessary to enable them to harness the more powerful engine. All production Mk XIIs had clipped wings for improved roll rate at low altitude.

The Spitfire Mk XIV was optimised for the Griffon in the same way that the earlier Mk VIII had been more closely matched to the most powerful Merlins. Some 957 production Mk XIVs were built, with the type's finest hour coming in mid-1944, when its

OPPOSITE Flying MB882/EB-B, Flight Lieutenant Don Smith leads a gaggle of Spitfire XIIs for the camera on 14 April 1944. In the hands of V1 ace Flight Lieutenant Terry Spencer on 3 September 1944, MB882 claimed the Mk XII's last air-to-air victory. (No. 41 Squadron Records)

straight-line speed was used to counter the V1 flying bomb menace in air defence patrols over southeast England. Although the Griffon-engined marks lost some of the handling prowess of their Merlin predecessors, they could outpace the majority of Allied piston-engined fighters.

The final version of the Spitfire, the Mk 24, first flew on 13 April 1946 and two years later, almost 12 years after the Spitfire prototype's first flight, the last Spitfire rolled off the production line. Griffon Spitfires served with the RAF until 1957, with the last combat missions flown during the Malayan Emergency in 1954.

PHOTO-RECONNAISSANCE SPITFIRES

As early as August 1939, a forward-thinking RAF officer suggested that the traditional policy of using modified bombers for reconnaissance missions was flawed. Flying Officer Maurice 'Shorty' Longbottom observed that a small, high-performance aircraft even if it were unarmed to save weight, stood more chance of evading enemy anti-aircraft and fighter defences to return safely with its precious photographs, than did a large, slow bomber, however well armed.

With demand for Spitfire fighters unrelenting, it was only the obvious failure of the RAF's photographic-reconnaissance aircraft – typically Bristol Blenheims – at the outbreak of war that persuaded Fighter Command to give up two Mk I Spitfires for modification to the photographic-reconnaissance (PR) role. The aircraft were assigned to Heston, close to London, where Commander Sidney Cotton was establishing 'The Heston Flight', a secret PR unit that included Longbottom among its early members.

The Spitfires emerged minus guns and radios, but with a camera in each wing and their airframes carefully cleaned up to ensure high performance. Trials over enemy territory began on 18 November 1939 and quickly proved the type's worth. These early PR Spitfires were retrospectively designated PR.Mk IA when the longer-ranged PR.Mk IB appeared in January 1940. There followed a series of Mk I-based models, up to PR.Mk IG, with variously increased fuel loads, revised camera fits and optimisation for low- or high-altitude operations. In 1941, the PR variants IC to IG were redesignated as PR.Mk III to Mk VII, the surviving PR.Mks IA and IB aircraft having been modified to later standards by this time. The aircraft were also re-engined with the Merlin 45 of the Spitfire Mk V.

Just as the RAF required a new Spitfire variant to counter the Fw 190, so it needed a PR model with increased survivability against the German aircraft. While it waited for the PR.Mk XI, based on the Mk VIII fighter, to become available, 15 Mk IXs were stripped of their armament and re-equipped as PR.Mk IX reconnaissance aircraft, for service from November 1942.

In December 1942 the first of 471 PR.Mk XIs came off the production line, the type taking on much of the RAF reconnaissance burden, alongside the de Havilland Mosquito, in the build-up to D-Day in June 1944 and beyond. Ironically, the Mk XI had been on the front line for 12 months by the time the first of just 16 PR.Mk X high-altitude Spitfires with pressurised cockpits entered service. More of the low-altitude Spitfire PR.Mk XIIIs were produced, however, 26 emerging from conversions of PR.Mk VII and standard Mk I and Mk V airframes.

From November 1944 the Spitfire FR.Mk XIV replaced the PR.Mk XIII, its 'FR' designation referring to fighter-reconnaissance, since the aircraft added a fuselage-mounted oblique camera to its standard gun armament. Post-war there was an FR.Mk 18 equivalent of the FR.Mk XIV, albeit with standard wing tips, rather than the clipped wings of the wartime variant.

Last and most capable of the dedicated Spitfire reconnaissance models, the Griffon-engined PR.Mk XIX saw service in the final weeks of the war as the first of 225 examples arrived on the front line. The Spitfire PR.Mk XIX's pressurised cabin, based on that of the Mk X, was modified in production for improved pilot visibility – the earlier mark had been criticised for its less than perfect canopy – and such was its high-altitude performance that a well-flown PR.Mk XIX could easily evade an Me 262 jet at height.

ABOVE/RIGHT Spitfire IA of No. 234 Squadron. (Osprey Publishing)

TECHNICAL DESCRIPTION

From the time the Spitfire entered service in the autumn of 1938, it underwent continuous modification aimed at enhancing its usefulness as a combat aircraft.

SPITFIRE I

The jig-built Spitfire I differed significantly from the hand-built K5054 in a number of key areas, primarily internally. The fighter's distinctive elliptical wing had been considerably strengthened so as to raise its never-to-be-exceeded speed from 380mph to 470mph. Flap travel was increased from 57° to 90°, and fuel tankage boosted from 75 to 84Imp gal. Other equipment and minor changes were also introduced,

resulting in the first production Spitfire I weighing 5,819lb fully loaded – 460lb heavier than K5054.

The first 64 airframes were fitted with the Merlin II engine, while the remaining Spitfire Is were powered by the 1,030hp Merlin III. From the 78th airframe onwards, the Rolls-Royce engine drove a three-bladed de Havilland or Rotol two-pitch or constant speed propeller, rather than the Watts two-bladed fixed-pitch wooden airscrew. The new

SPITFIRE MK IA SPECIFICATION

Powerplant: 1,030hp Merlin III V12 inline piston engine

Length: 29ft 11in (9.1m)

Height: 12ft 8in (3.8m)

Wing span: 36ft 10in (11.2m)

Wing area: 242ft^2 (22.4m^2)

Empty weight: 4,517lb (2,048kg)

Maximum take-off weight: 5,844lb (2,650kg)

Maximum speed at 15,000ft: 346mph (556km/h)

Range: 415 miles (667km)

Climb: to 20,000ft (6,096m) in 7.42 min

Service ceiling: 30,500ft (9,296m)

Armament: 8 x .303in machine guns

OPPOSITE The Spitfire I's eight guns, and associated ammunition bays, were covered by 22 panels secured by 150 half-turn Dzus fasteners. It was estimated that a proficient four-man re-arming team could turn a Spitfire around in 30 minutes. This No. 602 'City of Glasgow' Squadron aircraft was photographed at Drem, in East Lothian, in April 1940.

propeller shortened take-off run from 420 yards to 225 yards, increased the rate of climb, boosted top speed from 361mph to 365mph and made the Spitfire much easier to handle in combat. The first Spitfire Is reached No. 19 Squadron in August 1938, and further modifications were introduced following the early months of service flying.

Engine start problems were cured with a more powerful starter motor, an engine-driven hydraulic system replaced the hand pump that was originally used to raise and lower the undercarriage and the bulged canopy was introduced. Early in World War II, once it became clear that pilots of modern fighters needed armour protection, the previously unarmoured Spitfire I had a thick slab of laminated glass fitted to its windscreen. A .12in-thick light alloy cover was also fitted over the upper fuel tank in the fuselage, and 75lb of steel armour was installed behind and beneath the pilot's seat.

In the spring of 1940, the RAF introduced 100-octane fuel and the Spitfire I's Merlin engine

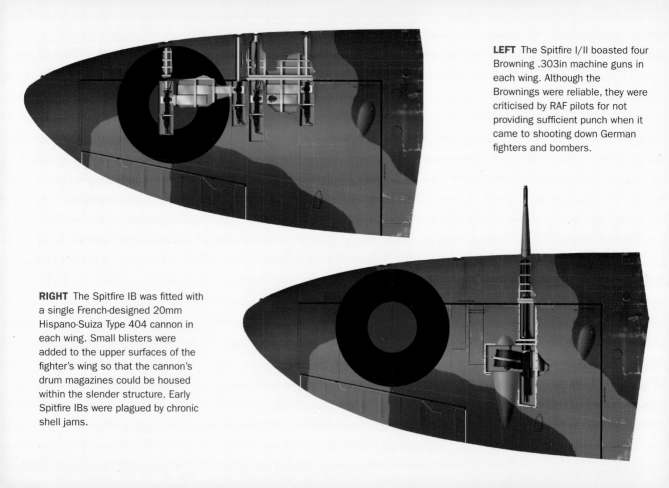

LEFT The Spitfire I/II boasted four Browning .303in machine guns in each wing. Although the Brownings were reliable, they were criticised by RAF pilots for not providing sufficient punch when it came to shooting down German fighters and bombers.

RIGHT The Spitfire IB was fitted with a single French-designed 20mm Hispano-Suiza Type 404 cannon in each wing. Small blisters were added to the upper surfaces of the fighter's wing so that the cannon's drum magazines could be housed within the slender structure. Early Spitfire IBs were plagued by chronic shell jams.

had to be modified to use this petrol. The higher octane allowed pilots to select double the supercharger boost for a maximum of five minutes (raising top speed by up to 34mph) without the risk of damaging the engine. IFF transponder equipment was also introduced soon after the outbreak of war, allowing radar operators on the ground to identify the aircraft they were tracking on their plots. Finally, just prior to the Battle of Britain, all frontline Spitfires were fitted with 'two-step' rudder pedals, with the upper step 6in higher than the lower step. Before entering combat, the pilot lifted his feet on to the upper steps, thus giving his body a more horizontal posture, which raised his blackout threshold by about 1G, allowing him to sustain tighter turns.

In the summer of 1940, non-Castle Bromwich-built aircraft that were still equipped with eight Browning .303in machine guns were redesignated Spitfire IA to differentiate them from the recently introduced cannon-armed Spitfire IB. Production of the Spitfire I ran from April 1938 through to March 1941, by which time 1,567 had been built.

SPITFIRE V

The Spitfire V was simply a Mk I airframe fitted with the new Merlin 45, 46, 50 or 50A engine. In the Merlin 45, the second stage of the Merlin XX's supercharger was removed and a new single-speed, single-stage supercharger fitted in its place. The Merlin 45 was rated at 1,440hp on take-off and was easy to mass produce. Other improvements included a new carburettor, which allowed for negative-G manoeuvres with no interruption of fuel flow to the engine.

Pilots soon found the Merlin 45-powered Spitfire V ran at excessively high oil temperatures. The original engine cooling system of the Spitfire I was not powerful enough, so a larger matrix had to be fitted to the cooler, which in turn required a larger air intake – the new oil cooler intake was enlarged and made circular in shape. The Spitfire I's fabric ailerons were also replaced with units in light alloy. The first Spitfire Vs were fitted with the A-type wing and increased armour plating, weighing in at 129lb. Top speed for the Spitfire VA was 375mph at 20,800ft and just 94 were built.

The Spitfire VB would ultimately be the most-produced Mk V variant. It featured the B-type wing, housing two Hispano 20mm cannon, with 60 rounds per weapon, and four .303in Browning machine guns with 350 rounds per gun. Armour was increased in weight to 152lb.

Spitfire VA AB320 was converted into a Mk VB and then used as the prototype for the first fully tropicalised Mk V. The most visible modification was the addition of the prominent Vokes filter beneath the nose. A tropical radiator and oil cooler were also installed, and the aircraft had provision for an external slipper tank of 90Imp gal. Other internal changes included the addition of tropical survival gear. Air tests revealed that the Spitfire VB Trop, fitted with a Merlin 45 engine, had a top speed of 337.5mph at 17,400ft. Rate of climb was 2,145ft per minute, with a ceiling of 34,500ft. A total of 3,911 Spitfire VBs was built, 776 by Supermarine, 2,995 in Castle Bromwich and 140 by Westland.

SPITFIRE MK VB SPECIFICATION

Powerplant: 1,440hp Rolls-Royce Merlin 45/46/50 V12 inline piston engine

Length: 29ft 11in (9.11m)

Height: 11ft 5in (3.48m)

Wing span: 36ft 10in (11.23m)

Empty weight: 5,100lb (2,313kg)

Maximum take-off weight: 6,785lb (3,078kg)

Maximum speed: 374mph (602km/h)

Service ceiling: 37,000ft (11,280m)

Armament: 2 x 20mm cannon; 4 x .303in machine guns

SPITFIRE XIV

The Spitfire Mk XIV was a combination of the Mk VIII airframe, albeit much modified, and the Griffon

ABOVE The initial production versions of the Spitfire VA and VB were merely Mk Is and IIs fitted with a Merlin 45 engine. The Mk VC (production of which began in October 1941) featured a redesigned and strengthened airframe. It was also fitted with the C-type or 'universal' wing and a short spinner. Very few photographs exist of a Mk VC without a Vokes filter, as seen here, before production switched to the tropical version. (Courtesy of Donald Nijboer)

SPITFIRE MK XIVE SPECIFICATION

Powerplant: 2,050hp Rolls-Royce Griffon 65 V12 inline piston engine

Length: 32ft 8in (9.96m)

Height: 11ft (3.35m)

Wing span: 36ft 10in (11.23m)

Maximum loaded weight: 10,065lb (5,565kg)

Maximum speed: 439mph (707km/h)

Service ceiling: 43,000ft (13,110m)

Armament: 2 x 20mm cannon; 2 x .50in machine guns

ABOVE Mk XIVE MV266/EB-J of Squadron Leader John Shepherd, OC No. 41 Squadron, Twente, Holland, April 1945. (Osprey Publishing)

65 engine of 2,050hp, driving a five-bladed airscrew. It was intended for both high- and low-altitude operations and the Griffon 65 was fitted with a two-speed supercharger and an intercooler, and to offset the fighter's lengthened nose, its fin area was increased. This and other aerodynamic improvements greatly improved lateral control. The aircraft could be fitted with either a 'B' wing, mounting two 20mm

cannon and four .303in Browning machine guns, or the 'E' wing, introduced on late production Mk IXs, with two 20mm cannon and a pair of .50in Browning machine guns. Thus fitted, the Mk XIV's operational weight with full fuel and ammunition was 8,400lb – considerably more than the 5,300lb of the original Spitfire I.

Prototype testing was conducted on several converted Spitfire VIIIs, the first of which flew in January 1943. They boasted several aerodynamic modifications, including the larger fin and the moving inboard of the ailerons in an effort to improve lateral stability.

The Mk XIV was highly regarded by those who flew it. One pilot who met with success, including the destruction of an enemy jet, was Flight Lieutenant Derek Rake of No. 41 Squadron, who recalled:

The take off in the Mk XIV was a bit different to the earlier Merlin-powered Spits in that the power of the Griffon meant that you had to use full rudder and even aileron to counteract the torque, and so stay on the narrow PSP (pierced-steel planking) strips on take-off. We had to limit the boost to about +8lb until we were off the ground. Thereafter, we had to get used to adjusting the trim as we changed power and/or speed in the range of up to +18lb. This was of course particularly important when firing either air-to-air or air-to-ground, as speed increased or decreased. Any skidding played havoc with accuracy.

It was always comforting to me to know that the increased power of the Griffon would enable me to turn inside and/or out climb a Bf 109 or Fw 190. We did find, however, that the latest Fw 190D could get away from us by rolling on its back and going vertically downwards. In an attempt to combat this manoeuvre, we were allowed to increase the boost to +21lb. To do this we had to push the throttle through a thin piece of piano wire. The only time I tried this, when attempting to catch up with an

ABOVE The Spitfire VA was virtually indistinguishable from the Mk I and II. Equipped with the A-type wing, it featured the same exhaust stubs, canopy and de Havilland propeller as fitted to the early marks. In fact the only way to distinguish a Mk VA from a Spitfire I or II was by the larger oil cooler, with its deeper housing and circular air intake, located under the port wing. (Courtesy of Donald Nijboer)

Fw 190D in a dive, there was a tremendous clatter and my Spit felt as if it was going to shake itself to pieces. I managed to keep the engine going by throttling right back – using just enough power to limp back to Volkel. It transpired that a con-rod had come through the side of the engine. It was confidence building to realise how robustly the Griffon was built.

Another time – the day of the crossing of the Rhine on 24 April 1945 – we started the day at first light at 25,000ft, trying to ensure that the Luftwaffe's Me 262s did not dive-bomb our troops crossing the river. Later in the day we were down at low level looking for German tanks in a wood. I was hit in the port wing by ground fire and again had heavy vibration in the engine. After landing back at Volkel without any flaps or brakes, I discovered that one blade of the five-bladed propeller had been shot off. What an engine!

COMBAT OPERATIONS

The first documented action between a Spitfire I and a Bf 109E took place just south of Calais, late in the morning of 23 May 1940. With things going badly for the Allies, Prime Minister Winston Churchill had ordered that more Fighter Command squadrons be moved to France. Air Chief Marshal Dowding strongly resisted this order, instead ordering six No. 11 Group units to be moved to forward airfields along the English south coast. A number of squadrons previously not involved in the Battle of France would commence operations along the French coast from 16 May, including Spitfire-equipped Nos 54 and 74 Squadrons, which provided fighter cover and support for Allied forces withdrawing to Dunkirk.

On the morning of 23 May, Spitfires from No. 74 Squadron had engaged a Henschel Hs 126 observation

OPPOSITE The retreat from Dunkirk as depicted by the artist Charles Chundall. The evacuation of the BEF across the English Channel against the odds became a powerful rallying point for the British people and a story of defiance. This artwork shows the miracle of the little ships, along with the fighter cover provided by the RAF, who duelled with the Luftwaffe over the beaches. (IWM ART LD 305)

aircraft and shot it down. However, defensive fire from the aircraft had hit the radiator of one of the fighters and forced its pilot, Squadron Leader F. L. White, to land at nearby Calais-Marck airfield. The latter was under threat from advancing German troops, so it was decided that a rescue mission needed to be launched, involving a two-seat Miles Master trainer and two escorting Spitfires from No. 54 Squadron. Flying the latter were future aces pilot

ENGAGING THE ENEMY

In 1940, most fighters had enough ammunition for 12 to 15 seconds' worth of fighting, so the pilot had to be selective about what he chose to fire at, and when, with a careful judgement of distance and angle.

Most decisive fighter encounters ended within a few seconds of the attack commencing. One aircraft dived on another from behind or out of the sun ('Beware the Hun in the Sun' was a common adage in the RAF), opened fire for two or three seconds and then broke away – a classic aerial ambush known as the 'bounce'. However, if neither side had an initial advantage, then the fighters would 'dogfight' – the aim being to get on the opponent's tail. Speed and manoeuvrability were crucial in such an instance, with the tighter the turn, the greater the ability to get behind an opponent.

In *The Most Dangerous Enemy* Robert Bungay identified four key factors. The first was the pilot's ability to exploit his aircraft's performance to the maximum. Secondly, excellent eyesight was necessary, a skill some pilots sought to improve upon. 'Sailor' Malan used to fix on a dot on a wall, look away and then turn his head and see how quickly he could focus on it again. Thirdly, you had to be a good shot; indeed early experience with shotguns often characterised the famous aces. And of course pilots needed a certain mental ability – the courage to know how to overcome fear and attack aggressively. For those that succeeded in aerial combat, it was a life-changing experience.

officers Johnny Allen (who would be killed in action by Hauptmann Adolf Galland on 24 July 1940 – the first Spitfire downed by the German ace) and Al Deere.

Once over the French airfield, they were engaged by a number of Bf 109Es, but with the Master safely on the ground, the two Spitfire pilots entered combat and claimed three destroyed. Al Deere recalled:

This was my first real combat, and the first recorded combat of a Spitfire with a Bf 109. My abiding memory was the thrill of the action – there was no sense of danger at that early stage in the war. So much so that I stayed behind the second of the two Bf 109s that I encountered after I had run out of ammunition just to see if I could do so. I only broke off when petrol became a factor. My prolonged fight with this Bf 109 allowed me to assess the relative performance of the two aircraft.

In early engagements between the Hurricane and Bf 109 in France, the speed and climb of the latter had become legendary, and were claimed by many to be far superior to that of the Spitfire. I was able to refute this, and indeed was confident that, except in a dive, the Spitfire was superior in most other fields, and was vastly more manoeuvrable. My superior rate of climb was, however, due mostly to the type of Spitfire with which my squadron was equipped. We had the first Rotol constant-speed airscrews on which we had been doing trials when the fighting started. Other Spitfires were, at that stage, using a two-speed airscrew (either fully fine pitch or fully course), which meant they lost performance in a climb. The constant-speed unit changed its pitch as the engine revs went up.

There was a great deal of scepticism about my claim that the Spitfire was the superior fighter, but the big thing for me was that we shouldn't have any fear of the Bf 109 in combat.

THE BATTLE OF BRITAIN

For the second and last time in the Luftwaffe's history, the Battle of Britain would see virtually the entire frontline strength of Bf 109Es concentrated in one area – the Channel coast. These aircraft would be charged

SPITFIRE I VS BF 109E

Deere's experience on 23 May was the first recorded clash between the Spitfire and Bf 109, but it was not the first time that these machines had come up against one another in the air. On 22 November 1939, Feldwebel Karl Hier landed a Bf 109E-3 intact at an airfield in France, after he had become disorientated in thick fog. His Bf 109E was thoroughly tested by the Armée de l'Air, after which it was flown to the UK in May 1940 for trials at the RAE at Farnborough.

In a series of mock combats fought between the German fighter and a Spitfire I fitted with a two-speed airscrew, the Bf 109E was found to be superior in all aspects bar its manoeuvrability and turning circle. The margins reduced rapidly when the Spitfire was fitted with a constant-speed airscrew, however, as Al Deere proved over France later that month.

In level flight, the Spitfire had little trouble staying behind the Bf 109E, nor did a dive present the pursuer with many problems. When the Spitfire was being pursued in a turning fight at medium altitude, the trials proved that the RAF fighter was the superior aircraft. Thanks to its outstanding rate of roll, the Spitfire pilot could shake off the Bf 109E by performing a flick half-roll and quickly pulling out of the subsequent dive.

The Bf 109E drew praise from the RAF trials team for its excellent handling and response, good low-speed climb angle, gentle stall, lack of any tendency to spin and short take-off run. However, it was criticised for its control heaviness at the upper end of its speed range – the Spitfire was just as difficult to fly at around 400mph, losing any clear advantage in manoeuvrability that it enjoyed over the Bf 109E.

Dr Alfred Price, commenting on the results of this trial in *Spitfire At War*, noted:

> Overall, the Spitfire I and Bf 109E matched each other fairly evenly. If they fought, victory would almost invariably go to the side which was the more alert, which held the initiative, which understood the strengths and weaknesses of its opponent's aircraft, which showed better team work and which, in the last resort, could shoot the more accurately.

OPPOSITE 1630hrs on 30 August 1940, No. 603 Sqn's Flying Officer Brian Carbury sighted three Bf 109s near Canterbury. 'I attacked the rear aircraft, and the leading two aircraft turned for my tail. I got a good burst in and the propeller of the rear enemy aircraft stopped, started and finally stopped, with white vapour coming out behind... I veered off as other aircraft were closing in on me.' (Osprey Publishing)

ABOVE Spitfires and Bf 109Es were rarely seen together in such close proximity on the ground in 1940, but when Pilot Officer Bill Caister's Spitfire was damaged he was forced to down his aircraft in France.

with achieving aerial supremacy as the German Kampfgeschwader and Stukageschwader strived to knock out Fighter Command in preparation for the seaborne invasion of southern England, codenamed Operation *Sealöwe* (Sea Lion).

Historians generally divide the Battle of Britain into four phases, commencing in early July 1940 with *Kanalkampf* (Channel Battle). During this period, German aircraft probed British defences primarily through attacks on coastal convoys, as well as port facilities on the south coast. The first major attack occurred on 4 July when 33 Junkers Ju 87 Stukas appeared above Portland, Dorset, and dived on the assembled convoys and naval installations. No British fighters could be scrambled in time to counter the raid. Over the following week both German and British losses mounted as the German raids gained in intensity. The Battle of Britain officially began on 10 July, although this did not signify a change in German policy but rather a reaction on the part of Fighter Command. That day saw the largest dogfight yet, as RAF fighters sought to protect convoys in the Channel. By the end of the day seven RAF fighters had been lost to the Luftwaffe's 13.

Fighter Command scored a great success on 12 August, when Spitfires from Nos 609 and 152 Squadrons were scrambled to intercept a group of German bombers. The Bf 109 fighter escorts, not believing that the small number of Spitfires was the main attack, maintained their higher altitude, staying there until ten bombers had been shot down. *Kanalkampf* would last until 12 August, and although

Fighter Command succeeded in matching the Luftwaffe in trying circumstances, it had suffered significant losses – including 27 Spitfires destroyed and 51 damaged. Many of these had been claimed by Bf 109E pilots seeking out RAF fighters in Freie Jagd (free hunt) sweeps independent of the bombers.

Tuesday 13 August was dubbed *Adlertag* (Eagle Day) by the Luftwaffe, and it signalled the start of the sustained campaign against RAF airfields, radar stations and other key military targets such as aircraft and aeroengine factories. During 11 days of sustained attacks, which saw both sides suffer heavy losses, the Luftwaffe hoped to assert its dominance through sheer weight of numbers. Certainly the Luftwaffe enjoyed some success on Eagle Day and immediately afterwards, when a number of the more inexperienced RAF pilots were lost. However, all three of the major raids that day were picked up by radar and intercepted. Although runways were damaged, they were quickly made operational again and key radar stations were usually back up-and-running in a matter of hours.

Eagle Day was designed to be the beginning of the end of Fighter Command. In this respect, the Luftwaffe did not even come close to success.

The following days saw further Luftwaffe attacks, including extensive raids on 15 August, 'Black Thursday'. While small 'distraction' raids were carried out on the south coast, the main bombing force was headed for Yorkshire. Hugh Dundas was with No. 616 Squadron, based at Leconsfield. His unit hadn't been in action since Dunkirk and he recalled the urgent scramble call:

> We were sitting in the mess on that day, actually at 30 minutes' notice, when the tannoy went, telling us in rather urgent tones to come to readiness... we put down our knives and forks, rushed out to get into the cars and pushed off down to the field as quickly as we could. When we got there the operations clerk was

jumping up and down for us to take-off as fast as we could individually, just to get airborne. Off we all went in ones and twos. We were told on the R/T that there was a large force of German bombers, indeed of Dornier 17s, which were aiming for Driffield. We had quite a field day that day and succeeded in shooting down quite a few of those wretched aeroplanes, which of course hadn't got any escort and were in broad daylight, without any loss to ourselves.

The British fighters claimed 14 enemy aircraft for no losses, and although ten aircraft of Bomber Command were destroyed on the ground, there was little other damage.

The incessant sorties, patrols and dogfights were beginning to take their toll on the British pilots in No. 11 Group, however, as Al Deere recalled:

> You were either at readiness or you were in the air. It was pretty tiring. I was bloody tired, I can tell you; very tired. My squadron, 54 I think, were down to five of

the original pilots, so we were operating on a bit of a shoestring, all new pilots...

You'd go for days, for example, without actually seeing the mess in daylight... If we were operating from the forward base, Manston, which we generally were up till towards the end, we'd be off before first light, so we'd be landing at first light at Manston. Similarly we'd come back in the evenings at last light. The rest of the time was spent either sitting at dispersal, which was way out the other side of the airfield, with a tent or a telephone, or in the air. We used to have our meals brought out to us... Never saw the public, never got off the airfield.

Between 24 August and 6 September, often considered the most dangerous days of the battle, the Germans continued to target Fighter Command airfields and aircraft factories, with growing success. The RAF would later call this 'the critical period' of the Battle of Britain, as it found losses ever harder to replace, stretching the pilots and their aircraft to the limits of their endurance.

Yet despite suffering serious casualties (136 Spitfires were lost in August alone), Fighter Command was in turn inflicting heavier losses on German forces. Indeed, Bf 110 Zerstörer (Destroyer) and Ju 87 Stuka Gruppen had been so badly affected that they would play little part in the rest of the campaign.

Critically, Reichsmarschall Hermann Göring questioned the tactics of continuing to attack radar stations when the British had so many, and he was also explicit in his order that airfields which 'had been successfully attacked one day should not be attacked the following day', presumably because he regarded it as a waste of effort. With this, Göring virtually guaranteed the continued operational capabilities of the frontline Spitfire and Hurricane squadrons.

In contrast to Göring's amateurish interference, British Spitfire pilots were still under the command of Air Chief

OPPOSITE An armourer re-arms a Spitfire at RAF Fowlmere, while the pilot speaks with the mechanic. During the battle, ground crews would work against the clock to ready the fighters. (IWM CH 1458)

Marshal Hugh Dowding. He had been responsible for introducing the 'Dowding system' whereby radar, raid plotting and radio control of aircraft were integrated. In the hands of this dedicated professional, ably assisted by Air Vice-Marshal Keith Park, commander of No. 11 Fighter Group, the British enjoyed a distinct advantage despite the scores of German bombers and fighters increasingly darkening the skies over south-east England.

Through navigational error, the Luftwaffe had dropped a handful of bombs on London and the RAF launched a reprisal raid upon Berlin over the night of 25/26 August. Little damage was done, but Hitler gave Reichsmarschall Göring free rein to retaliate and on 7 September his forces targeted London; it was a decisive error that allowed Fighter Command to recuperate relatively unmolested. The first enemy aircraft were spotted at 4pm, and radar screens lit up as wave after wave of enemy machines crossed the Channel. It was a fearsome sight – almost 350 bombers accompanied by 617 Bf 109s and 110s. Nothing had been seen like it before, and the vast formation advanced towards London. Unprepared for this type of attack, Fighter Command was slow to respond, but when it did arrive, 38 German bombers and fighters were shot down, for the loss of 28 British aircraft.

Later the capital was attacked both by day and night, culminating in two massive daylight raids (involving more than 250 bombers and 300+ Bf 109Es) on 15 September – immortalised thereafter as Battle of Britain Day. Vast numbers of RAF fighters took to the sky in defence.

By now the Jagdflieger were forbidden from flying their favoured Freie Jagd sorties, ranging far and wide in front of the bombers. Instead, Göring ordered them to provide close formation escort for the bombers, which had suffered growing losses to the seemingly indestructible RAF. As if to prove that Fighter

OPPOSITE Pilots between sorties would grab a few precious minutes of relaxation when they could, as dogfighting was both mentally and physically draining. Here pilots of No. 610 Squadron are shown relaxing at RAF Hawkinge in July 1940 still wearing their 'Mae West' lifejackets. (IWM HU 1062)

Command did indeed still have plenty of fight left in it, both waves of bombers were met by close to 300 Hurricanes and Spitfires. In what would prove to be one of the final large-scale raids made by the Luftwaffe during the campaign, 19 Bf 109Es were shot down. Fighter Command lost seven Spitfires and 20 Hurricanes on 15 September, in contrast to the Luftwaffe's 56 aircraft.

The Battle of Britain officially ended on 31 October, by which time 610 Bf 109Es had been lost in combat – a little more than one-third of the Luftwaffe's total losses of 1,792 aircraft. During the same period, Fighter Command had seen 361 of its Spitfires destroyed. Both the Spitfire I/II and the Bf 109E would continue to clash in the skies over England and, increasingly, occupied Europe, through to the end of 1941, but the battle to prevent the fall of Britain, like the fall of France several months earlier, was over.

LEFT Luftwaffe bomber crews being briefed prior to a mission. (IWM MH 5321)

AFTER THE BATTLE

As 1940 ended, more and more Hurricane units were now switching to Spitfires – often battle-tired Mk Is, but also newer Mk IIs and the significantly improved Mk V. By then the tactics being employed by Spitfire squadrons in the front line had also altered dramatically from those in place for much of the Battle of Britain. Several units had taken it upon themselves to modify the formations they flew when going into combat, and at the forefront of these changes was Spitfire-equipped No. 74 Squadron. Its CO, Squadron Leader 'Sailor' Malan, was one of the best tacticians in the RAF. He had claimed nine Bf 109Es destroyed during 1940, so his theories on fighter formations had been formulated through bitter combat experience.

During the final stages of the Battle of Britain, Malan began dividing his 12-aircraft formations into three sections of four, rather than the traditional four sections of three, in an unwieldy 'vic'. Now, if a formation of Spitfires broke up after being bounced, its four-aircraft sections would split into two fighting pairs, which operated similarly to the German Rotte. With the three section leaders flying in a widely-spaced 'V', and the rest of their sections in line astern behind them, Malan's formation now possessed mutual support, coverage of blind spots to the rear and cohesion if forced to turn in combat. The loose line-astern formation was also much easier to fly than tight 'Battle Formation', thus freeing pilots to devote most of their time to looking out for the enemy, rather than watching what their section leader was up to.

THE *CIRCUS*

Fighter Command and the Jagdwaffe continued to lock horns regularly until the end of 1940. However, the RAF soon went from being on the defensive in 1940 to taking the fight to the Germans in 1941. In the vanguard of this campaign was Fighter Command, whose new commander-in-chief, Air Chief Marshal Sir Sholto Douglas, wanted his squadrons 'leaning forward into France'. Two pilots from Spitfire-equipped No. 66 Squadron had actually performed the first such mission

on 20 December 1940, when they strafed Le Touquet. This was the first time Spitfires had sortied over France since the fall of Dunkirk.

Large-scale operations aimed at enticing the Jagdwaffe into combat over France and the Low Countries commenced in earnest in January 1941, with the first *Circus* mission taking place on the 10th of the month. Spitfire units from Nos 10 and 11 Groups were heavily involved in this long-running offensive from the very start. These were daylight attacks performed by a small group of bombers escorted by a dozen squadrons of fighters. The primary objective was to draw the German fighters into the air and inflict casualties; destruction of targets was of secondary importance.

With operations progressing ever deeper into occupied Europe, the short-ranged Spitfire was finding it difficult to offer the vulnerable medium bombers the protection

LEFT A still from a camera gun taken from the Supermarine Spitfire Mark I of No. 609 Squadron flown by Pilot Officer R. F. G. Miller on 25 September 1940. This shows a Heinkel He III receiving hits in the port engine from Miller's machine guns. (IWM CH 1830)

they required. Thus the Spitfire II Long Range saw considerable service from the spring of 1941, flying with no fewer than eight units, as aircraft were passed between squadrons rotating in and out of No. 11 Group.

By June 1941, six RAF fighter squadrons had converted to Spitfire Vs, or were in the process of doing so. That same month saw the German invasion of the Soviet Union, and eager to support his new ally, Churchill assured the Soviet government that he would do all he could to hold German forces down in the west. This forced the RAF to adopt an even more aggressive stance over occupied Europe, and further *Circus* operations began.

Typical of these operations was *Circus* No. 62, when six Bristol Blenheims were to attack the power station in Lille on 7 August, covered by no fewer than 18 squadrons of Spitfires and two of Hurricanes. Six of the squadrons operated Mk Vs, while four were in the process of re-equipping and so flew both the Mk V and their older Mk IIs. Those squadrons with older Spitfire variants were to provide escort cover. Only a few German fighters came up to harry the main raiding force, and the after-action report from the Tangmere Wing, led by Wing Commander Douglas Bader, described the scrappy combats that followed:

Wing met over base, crossed the English coast over Hastings at 23/24/25,000 feet and made landfall over Le Touquet at 23/24/27,000 ft. A large orbit was made between Merville and Le Touquet. Proceeded towards the target area, encountering many Me 109s approximately 1,000ft above. Enemy aircraft came down out of the sun on the starboard quarter – the Wing turned to attack and the enemy aircraft dived away refusing to engage, but dogfights ensued. These tactics ensued over the Hazebrouck, Merville and Lille areas and on the way back to the French coast where the 109s broke away. The coast was recrossed by squadrons separately between Le Touquet and Boulogne; all the pilots and aircraft had returned by 18.55, with the exception of one from No. 41 Squadron.

Circus No. 62 illustrates well the difficulties involved for Fighter Command in performing these missions. The German fighter force could choose when, where and whether to engage the raiding force, and when it did engage, it invariably did so on terms that gave its fighters the best possible chance to inflict losses at the lowest possible cost. Expressed merely in terms of aircraft destroyed on each side, the *Circus* operations were not, and were unlikely ever to be, a success for the RAF. Yet the political imperative dictated that German day fighter units be held back in the west, and the *Circus* was the RAF's chosen instrument for doing so. There was a further consideration. In war a fighter force needs opportunities to fight or its morale, its fighting spirit and its fighting capability will wither away. By sending units on frequent offensive operations over enemy territory,

Sir Sholto Douglas ensured that Fighter Command remained an effective force during the difficult years of 1941–42.

THE BATTLE FOR MALTA

Virtually all Spitfire I/IIs had either been relegated to Training Command or rebuilt as Mk VBs by December 1941. Later marks of Spitfire would, of course, continue to take the fight to the Jagdwaffe, duelling with improved versions of the Axis aircraft to help the Allies ultimately claim final victory in Europe in World War II, as can clearly be seen in the defence of Malta only a year later.

Some 17 long months had passed since the end of the Battle of Britain, and the Spitfire was now seeing service outside the British Isles. For example, as March 1942 drew to a close, 31 Spitfire VBs had been added to Malta's defences to counter the Luftwaffe's build-up in Sicily. By early April the Luftwaffe had close to 400 aircraft ready to deploy from the island. Up to that point Malta's aerial defenders had made do with a mixed bag of Gladiators, Hurricanes and Fairey Fulmars. The island's commanders,

OPPOSITE No. 72 Squadron Spitfire IIAs form up off the Kent coast in the summer of 1941 prior to heading across the Channel on yet another *Circus* over France. The unit is still operating in 'vics' of three here, although the aircraft have closed up especially for the photographer, strapped into a Blenheim bomber.

while grateful for the Spitfire's long-awaited arrival, were still extremely anxious after intelligence reports indicated that Hitler intended to seize Malta by the end of April in order to safeguard the Mediterranean sea lanes for Rommel's new desert offensive.

The Joint Intelligence Sub Committee of the Chiefs-of-Staff reported to the British government that Malta's weakened state made it ripe for invasion. To add to the defenders' distress, the first of 52 brand new Regia Aeronautica (Italian Air Force) Macchi C.202 Folgores from 9° and 10° Gruppi, 4° Stormo had been flown into Sicily to commence offensive operations. The arrival of 4° Stormo greatly increased the size of the Axis fighter force, putting even more pressure on Malta's dwindling defences.

By the third week of April punishing raids by Luftwaffe and Regia Aeronautica units had reduced the number of serviceable Spitfires and Hurricanes on Malta to a mere handful. On the 19th, seven more Hurricanes arrived from North Africa, these being the first RAF fighters seen in the air over the island in five days. The initial batch of Spitfires delivered during March had brought some relief, but there had been too few of them to conduct any sustained combat operations. Help was on the way, however.

On 1 April, Prime Minister Churchill had cabled US President Franklin D. Roosevelt directly and pressed his case for assistance in getting Spitfires to Malta. Using the US Navy carrier USS *Wasp*, the RAF would be able to deliver 50 Spitfires to the island. Roosevelt agreed, and on 20 April Operation *Calendar* succeeded, with the delivery of 46 Spitfires. The surprising and sudden arrival of so many aircraft breathed new life into the defences, although this would again be only a temporary fix.

The Regia Aeronautica and Luftwaffe responded later that same day by mounting 272 bomber sorties against Malta's three airfields – Takali, Luqa and Hal Far. While the Italian side of the mission was aborted due to a mid-air collision between two C.202s, the persistent Luftwaffe attacks took a heavy toll. By 21 April only 27 Spitfires were still flyable, and this figure was reduced to 17 during the course of the day. Air Vice-Marshal Sir Hugh Lloyd,

ENGAGING THE ENEMY: MALTA

During the defence of Malta the Spitfires generally used the 'B' armament, and while the initial Mk VC Trops had been delivered with a 'C' arrangement, two of the cannon were soon taken out due to frequent jamming caused by faulty ammunition. Pilots also noted improved performance with two cannon removed. The Hispano had a useful range of 600 yards for air-to-air fighting, with a total firing time of between ten and 12 seconds, while the machine guns could be fired for a further five seconds. The low weight-of-fire and slight penetration of the .303in shells meant that pilots had to open fire at extremely close range to do any serious damage.

While the Spitfire is regarded as one of the best fighters of World War II, there is good reason to infer that it was not the best gun platform. Weapons that were easily harmonised when jacked up in the hangar would be subject to a number of twisting forces while airborne. Propeller torque, engine vibration and the lightness of the Spitfire's structure led to torsional flexing of the fuselage and flying surfaces. At high power settings precise sighting would be lost, along with the ability to score first-round strikes at ranges beyond 200 yards. Weapon harmonisation was also an issue, as the machine guns were not harmonised with the cannon. Rather than being set to converge at a point ahead of the gunsight, they were aligned to fill a volume of air in front of the fighter with as much lead as possible.

Air-Officer-Commanding (AOC) Malta, was not impressed. After a quick inspection of the newly delivered Spitfires following the events of the 21st, he found the condition of many of them left much to be desired. Guns were dirty and had not been fired since they were installed in the UK and many radios were not working. Lloyd's harshest critique, however, fell on the new pilots. In his message to HQ Fighter Command he said bluntly, 'Only fully experienced operational pilots must come here. It is no place for beginners. Casualties up to now have been the beginners.'

The heavy attacks on the three RAF airfields would continue unabated throughout the rest of April, with devastating results. By the end of April just seven Spitfires and a handful of Hurricanes remained serviceable. All three airfields had been savagely pounded, with Takali

OPPOSITE 9 May 1942 would see the year's largest delivery of Spitfires to Malta when, as part of Operation *Bowery*, *Eagle* and *Wasp* launched 64 Spitfires between them – 61 fighters arrived safely on Malta. Twenty of the Spitfire Mk VC Trops embarked in the US Navy carrier can be seen here below deck in *Wasp's* cavernous hangar bay. (Courtesy of Donald Nijboer)

receiving 841 tons of bombs alone. The defending fighters were credited with 53 victories during the month.

The Allied reinforcement of Malta from the air would continue, nevertheless. Flying off the carriers USS *Wasp* and HMS *Eagle* on 9 May, 61 fighters would make it safely to the island. This time the Malta-based personnel were better prepared for their new arrivals. Once on the ground, individual aircraft would make for their assigned aircraft pen. There, five groundcrew would immediately strip the Spitfire of its long-range tank and refuel it. A replacement pilot would then strap into the fighter and immediately take to the air. This new system worked well, for despite there being nine Axis raids on fighter bases on Malta that day, no Spitfires were destroyed on the ground.

Saturday, 9 May was undoubtedly one of the most successful days in the defence of Malta. Sixty-one Spitfires had arrived safely and during the frenetic fighting that followed their arrival, only four had been shot down, with six more damaged on the ground. By nightfall, counting the Spitfires already on the island, the defenders had at least 50 Supermarine fighters, and a handful of Hurricanes,

ready for operations on 10 May. In turn, the Axis units had suffered modest losses.

That next day was critical in the defence of Malta. No fewer than five Spitfire squadrons (Nos 126, 185, 249, 601 and 603) were ready for battle on the morning of 10 May, and as the first raid approached the island the defenders reacted like never before. No longer resigned to sending just a handful of fighters into the fray, the RAF scrambled 37 Spitfires and 13 Hurricanes, and the day saw the first confirmed destruction of a C.202 by a Spitfire.

After several Luftwaffe raids by Ju 87s and Ju 88s, the Regia Aeronautica put in an appearance at just gone 6pm when five CANT Z.1007bis, with an escort of 20 C.202s from 4° Stormo and ten Reggiane Re.2001s from 2° Gruppo, approached the island. German Ju 87s followed the Italian aircraft in, with a large escort of Bf 109s. To meet the threat, 42 Spitfires were scrambled, with aircraft from No. 601 Squadron being the first to attack. Within minutes a Z.1007bis had been shot down, as had the C.202 of Capitano Roberto Dagasso, CO of 97ª

Squadriglia. He had fallen victim to New Zealander Pilot Officer Wally Caldwell of No. 601 Squadron.

By dusk on 10 May, the Spitfire pilots had claimed three Ju 88s, nine Ju 87s, two Bf 109s, one Z.1007bis and one C.202 destroyed – these successes were very similar to the losses admitted by the Axis units. In return, the Italian fighter pilots claimed six RAF fighters shot down. However, only three Spitfires had been lost that day (none to C.202s), with six more slightly damaged. The Italians exacted some revenge for their losses on 14 May, when three Spitfires were credited to pilots from 2° and 9° Gruppi, and Australian ace Sergeant 'Tony' Boyd of No. 185 Squadron was shot down and killed.

The greatest number of C.202s shot down to date was

OPPOSITE Blast pens were vital for the survival of fighter aircraft on the ground. Those on Malta were made with various materials – the ones seen here at Takali, protecting two Spitfire VCs from No. 229 Squadron, were made out of sand bags. Others were constructed from empty fuel cans or limestone blocks recovered from bombed-out buildings. The extreme wear and tear of combat can clearly be seen on Spitfire EP691 in the foreground, which had been flown into Malta on 17 August 1942. (Frederick Galea)

on 15 May, when 30 Folgores from 4° Stormo were escorting three Savoia-Marchetti S.84bis bombers targeting the Fort Campbell barracks in St Paul's Bay at 9.15am. They were intercepted by 12 Spitfires from Nos 249 and 603 Squadrons and in the resulting dogfight the Italians claimed four Spitfires shot down, although there were actually no losses on the British side. Number 249 Squadron's Pilot Officer Lawrie Verrall fired an accurate burst into the Macchi flown by Capitano Alberto Argenton, commander of 91ª Squadriglia, who was killed when the fighter hit the sea.

A few hours later a single reconnaissance Ju 88, and its Bf 109 and C.202 escorts, was engaged off the island. Future Australian ace Sergeant Jack Yarra of No. 603 Squadron took on the escort screen, noting in his Combat Report, 'Engaged seven 109s, damaged leader, was attacked by four 202s. Shot down one, who collided with his No. 2. Fought the remaining two until out of ammo'. Three days later Yarra would 'make ace' when he claimed two Bf 109s shot down. The newly arrived Spitfires were making their presence felt.

Despite the significant losses of 10 May, Feldmarschall Albert Kesselring, Luftwaffe Commander-in-Chief, South, convinced himself that Malta was no longer a threat. Having informed Hitler that the Luftwaffe and the Regia Aeronautica had suffered only modest losses in the recent blitz on the island, Kesselring was told to reduce air operations over Malta and begin the transfer of aerial assets to North Africa and the Eastern Front.

In mid-May three Jagdgeschwader would be transferred out, along with a number of bomber units. The Regia Aeronautica was also anxious to increase its strength in North Africa, duly ordering 4° Stormo to Libya. To compensate for this move, 155° Gruppo, 51° Stormo was transferred to Sicily from Rome. On 18 May, Maggiore Duilio Fanali led the Gruppo's three squadriglie (351ª, 360ª and 378ª Squadriglie) to Gela.

OPPOSITE Success and survival in aerial combat often came down to the simple act of spotting the enemy first, and for a young recruit this was probably the most important lesson to learn, and practise, before heading into combat. This dramatic Air Ministry vision training poster is succinct and unambiguous. (Courtesy of Donald Nijboer)

RESTRICTED) FOR OFFICIAL USE ONLY

HE WHO SEES FIRST LIVES LONGEST

Systematic
SCANNING
is essential

VISION TRAINING FOR AIRCREWS   A.D. 2824 SHEET 4

R.T.P   Nº 51-1313 H5&5

Seventeen more Spitfires arrived on Malta on the 18th as part of Operation *LB*, these machines flying off *Eagle*, and in June there was a rotation of Spitfire pilots to the island, along with 213 new Mk Vs. However, by mid-June it was clear that Malta would not fall to aerial assault; the other options for its defeat were blockade or invasion and both of these were beyond the resources available. As such, Axis bombing continued throughout June in the form of low-level attacks and fighter sweeps. In July, further Axis units were transferred to Italy as part of a new offensive and attacks on Malta focused on the airfields – the Spitfire squadrons were scrambled to meet them head on.

By mid-July the Italian offensive had run out of steam. Regia Aeronautica bombers stopped appearing over Malta and the fighter force struggled to sustain operations. On 27 July the C.202 units were dealt a demoralising blow.

Thirteen C.202s were assigned to escort nine Ju 88s, and 22 Spitfires from Nos 185, 249 and 126 Squadrons were scrambled to intercept the formation. RAF ace Sergeant Beurling was among the Spitfire pilots who attacked the Italian fighters, almost immediately claiming a C.202 destroyed when he shot its engine and radiator. He then moved onto his next target and opened fire, recalling: 'The poor devil simply blew to pieces in the air'. His victim was Capitano Furio Doglio Niclot, the leading Italian ace of the Malta campaign.

October would see a renewed effort over Malta from the Germans and Italians in what would prove to be the final attempts made to neutralise the island. Known as the 'October Blitz', this intense period of combat began on the 11th and ended just a week later.

During the attacks the Axis launched 2,400 sorties and dropped 440 tons of bombs, but no airfields were put out of action for longer than 30 minutes, and, on average, 74 Spitfires were ready to oppose each attack. By the end of October the battle for Malta was all but over.

OPPOSITE Above Malta, the RAF Spitfires duelled with the Luftwaffe and Italians for control of the skies, repeatedly engaging in aerial dogfights. (Osprey Publishing)

ABOVE Once foe now friend, this ex-RAF Spitfire VC Trop – photographed here at Galatina parked alongside the damaged wing of a Spitfire – was one of 53 ex-RAF Supermarine fighters issued to 20° Gruppo, 51° Stormo of the Aeronautica Co-Belligerante in October 1944. (Richard J. Caruana)

AFTER THE BATTLE

The Spitfire V and C.202 would continue to meet in combat after the 'October Blitz', although Operation *Torch* and the Allied invasion of Tunisia and Algeria on 8 November 1942 all but ended enemy air activity over Malta. As soon as airfields could be secured in North Africa the RAF flew in seven units of Spitfire Vs (Nos 72, 81, 93, 11, 152, 154 and 242 Squadrons). The USAAF also contributed the Spitfire V-equipped 31st and 52nd Fighter Groups. Italian and German forces in North Africa were now facing total destruction. The Regia Aeronautica rushed what remaining C.202s it could spare to North Africa to help stem the tide, but by 21 February 1943 just 55 Folgores were serviceable on Sicily, split between 6° and 16° Gruppi.

The Axis surrender in North Africa on 13 May 1943 led directly to the invasion of Sicily (Operation *Husky*) on 10 July. Located just 60 miles from Sicily, Malta would play a major role in the invasion, with 23 squadrons of Spitfires providing fighter and fighter-bomber support. Although several units had re-equipped with the more powerful Spitfire VIII and IX by then, the Mk V remained the most numerous RAF fighter type in-theatre.

In response to the impending invasion, the Regia Aeronautica prepared its defence of the island. On the eve of *Husky*, the Italians could muster 359 airworthy aircraft, of which approximately 67 were C.202s. Outnumbered and outgunned, the C.202 pilots fought a losing battle. By 17 August the battle for Sicily was over and the bombing of mainland Italy increased in tempo. The fall of Sicily and the bombing of Rome ultimately led to a signed armistice with the Allies on 3 September 1943. A split in the Regia Aeronautica

followed, resulting in Italy having separate air forces fighting for either side.

In the south the Aeronautica Co-Belligerante was formed, but it suffered from a serious shortage of aircraft. In May 1944 the Allies agreed to re-equip the Italians with more modern aircraft types, and in an ironic twist, 20° Gruppo, 51° Stormo received 53 ex-RAF Spitfire VBs and VCs.

NORTH AFRICA
THE BATTLE

'Spitfires made ten sorties acting as high cover to Hurricanes. Flt Lt Sabourin and Sgt James attacked two ME 109s southwest of Tobruk. One ME 109 destroyed.' Thus, in the dry and prosaic language of the handwritten *Operational Record Book* (ORB) of No. 145 Squadron for 8 June 1942 did the diarist record the first victory of a Spitfire over the Western Desert. Joseph Sabourin, a 27-year-old Canadian who already had three victories to his name from flying Curtiss Tomahawks with No. 112 Squadron, and his wingman, Sergeant James, had shot down a Bf 109 over the desert some 15 miles southwest of Tobruk.

With the Luftwaffe achieving a degree of ascendancy over the RAF's Hurricanes, Tomahawks and Curtiss Kittyhawks in North Africa by early 1942, the despatch of Spitfire-equipped squadrons to Egypt was seen as a matter of urgency, despite demands elsewhere. Number 145 Squadron was an experienced Fighter Command unit and in mid-February 1942 it had left for the Middle East along with another experienced Spitfire squadron, No. 92. The end of April also saw No. 601 Squadron arrive in Egypt, having come via Malta, and it too began readying itself for renewed operations. By then, No. 145 Squadron had begun to receive its Spitfire VBs at Helwan, on the Nile, south of Cairo, where it had worked up as part of the Desert Air Force (DAF).

By May 1942, Generalfeldmarschall Erwin Rommel's Afrika Korps and his Italian allies had been steadily building up against the Allied front in Cyrenaica that ran from Gazala south through Bir Hacheim. On 24 May No. 145 Squadron had moved forward to Gambut,

between Tobruk and Bardia, and commenced flying defensive patrols. Two days later Rommel attacked Gazala, thus beginning six weeks of violent fighting on the ground and in the air that eventually resulted in a British retreat deep into Egypt.

The situation on the ground continued to deteriorate, with the British suffering heavy losses at Knightsbridge, pre-empting a withdrawal from the Gazala line, resulting in DAF squadrons 'leapfrogging' in an easterly direction. No. 145 Squadron flew intensively throughout, completing some 22 sorties on 16 June. The unit's diarist recorded the intensity of the air action the following day, as the battle reached its zenith:

Standing patrols over base were resumed and 18 sorties were made. Plt Off Weber encountered a Macchi 202 near Gambut and pursued it to Sidi Rezegh… Plt Off Hanley and Sgt Barker attacked two ME 109s and Flt Lt Monk and Plt Off Malins attacked two others. Plt Off Hanley and Sgt Barker provided a most inspiring spectacle as they chased the two MEs at a low altitude away from the aerodrome. The standing patrol was ended at 1705hrs… It is not possible to know how many enemy aircraft were destroyed by the squadron… The moral effect of the squadron's operations was considerable, and it was felt respectively by the enemy and the units we operated with against him. It was a new experience for Messerschmitt pilots to have to look up instead of down!

Despite much gallant fighting, the enemy's inexorable advance continued, and on the 21st Tobruk, so long a symbol of dogged resistance, surrendered. Its loss was a huge blow to Allied morale and prompted Rommel to continue his advance into Egypt; eventually leading to his assault on El Alamein, which saw heavy fighting.

Despite the ground fighting settling into an exhausted stalemate, the air fighting continued through June and July, and into August. On 1 August, No. 92 Squadron at last received its first Spitfire and became operational on the 13th, flying its first Spitfire patrol the following day when it ran into a big fight around a returning bomber formation. Appropriately, it was the CO, Squadron Leader Jeff Wedgewood, who opened the unit's account in the desert by hitting the cooling system of the Bf 109 flown by Leutnant Mix, who had to crash land and became a prisoner of war (PoW).

As the battle for El Alamein continued, aerial operations intensified through August, and on 7 September Bruce Ingram of No. 601 Squadron became the first Spitfire ace of the desert campaign. The decisive Battle of El Alamein opened with a massive artillery barrage on a narrow front during the evening of 23 October, and the three Spitfire units were out early the following morning covering fighter-bombers and countering enemy air attacks as Axis forces fiercely resisted the 'push'.

In succeeding days the RAF was committed to preventing any enemy attempt at concentrating forces and in interdicting supply lines, so there were innumerable combats fought. For example, during the afternoon of the 25th a quartet of Spitfires from No. 92 Squadron attacked two Bf 109s, one of which was shot down into the sea by

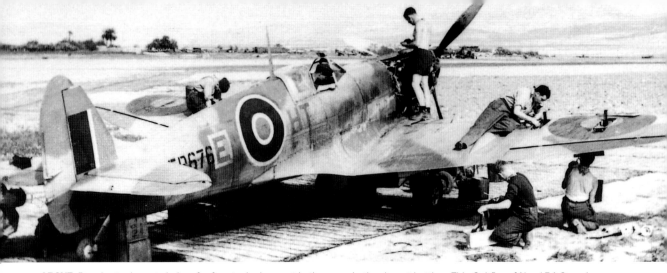

ABOVE Repairs to damaged aircraft often took place out in the open in the desert battles. This Spitfire of No. 154 Squadron was photographed on 24 April 1943, but was lost on a bomber escort mission the following day. (via Ashworth)

Flight Lieutenant John Morgan for his sixth victory. A short while later five more Bf 109s were attacked by a patrol from No. 145 Squadron, allowing Flight Lieutenant Cecil Saunders to claim his seventh, and last, success.

Finally, on 4 November, after further heavy fighting, the 8th Army began a general breakout and the race across the desert in pursuit of the Afrika Korps began. The speed of the withdrawal was breath-taking as both sides raced for Benghazi. Spitfire squadrons regularly moved forward during this period, taking off from Egyptian airfields and returning to newly captured landing grounds in Libya.

AFTER THE BATTLE

By the turn of the year the four Spitfire units had moved to, or were soon to arrive at, the desert strip at Alem El Chel, some 30 miles southeast of Sirte and deep into Libyan territory.

On 7 January, for the first time since El Alamein, No. 92 Squadron met enemy fighters in large numbers that stayed and fought, and two Bf 109s from II./JG 77 were destroyed. Climbing to 12,000ft, John Morgan claimed his eighth, and last, success. The other victory went to former US 'Eagle' squadron pilot Flight Officer Leo Nomis, but two Spitfires were also lost. Strafing attacks by Bf 109s and C.202s were repeated the next day, the first raid being intercepted at 8.15am by No. 145 Squadron and resulting in Flight Lieutenant Bert Houle shooting down a Messerschmitt. It was the Canadian's first victory in a Spitfire, but it elevated him to ace status:

> I got behind one which flew straight into the sun and fired a few bursts at him. The pilot panicked and turned down sun while diving for ground level. When he levelled out I was a few thousand feet above him, and I used my height to close the gap between us. When well within range, I pressed the firing button and two cannons and four machine guns started to register hits…

On 16 January Rommel issued the order to pull back, and as his forces headed for the Tunisian border they were constantly harassed by the DAF and advanced elements of the pursuing 8th Army. On the 22nd the last German troops evacuated Tripoli, leading to a curtailment of DAF operations.

NORTHWEST EUROPE

The Spitfire V would continue flying well into 1944. By the time of the D-Day landings on 6 June 1944, nine squadrons of LF.Mk Vs were assigned to the Air Defence of Great Britain (ADGB) organisation that had replaced Fighter Command in the home defence role, and two squadrons to the Air Spotting Pool. A host of other Spitfire marks was in use during the latter years of the war, and saw action across much of northwest Europe.

D-DAY AND INTO NORMANDY

The main task for ADGB before and immediately after D-Day was to protect the assembling invasion fleet from the prying eyes of Luftwaffe reconnaissance aircraft. This mission primarily fell to the high-altitude Spitfire VIIs, and in the early days of June Nos 131 and 616 Squadrons flew patrols providing top cover to the mass of shipping assembled in Lyme Bay and off Portland, for example. From Bradwell Bay No. 124 Squadron flew similar patrols over the Dover Strait, such as that flown by future ace Flight Lieutenant Peter Ayerst who logged daily patrols in the Spitfire VII, including three on 5 June 1944, the eve of D-Day.

That night at Tangmere at 11.30pm, Group Captain W. R. 'Iron Bill' MacBrien, commanding No. 126 Wing, told his assembled squadrons, 'This is it!'

On 6 June – D-Day – all night fighters were ordered to be clear of the Normandy assault area by 4.30am to allow the day fighters to take over responsibility, and through the day these aircraft flew more than 1,500 sorties, almost 900 of them by Spitfires. The fighters patrolled continuously at medium level, or below cloud, over all five beaches and inland to a depth of 5 miles. They also covered the vast assault fleet offshore, each squadron undertaking 50-minute low-level patrols.

First over the area, and the first ADGB fighters to witness the landings, were the Spitfire VBs of Nos 130, 501 and 611 Squadrons, a patrol from 126 Wing having taken off from Harrowbeer at 3.50am. It overflew *Omaha* and *Gold* beaches before returning shortly after 6am. After a hasty breakfast, the pilots were soon airborne on another patrol. Flying with No. 501 Squadron was Flight Lieutenant Warren Peglar, who described the scene:

> On the morning of 6 June I was sent on patrol, leading a flight of four Spitfires over *Juno* and *Sword* beaches. We were airborne at first light and the sight was absolutely awesome. We had become accustomed to flying over a vast and empty Channel, which was now filled with hundreds of ships, ploughing through some nasty, rainy weather and fairly heavy seas. When we arrived over the

beachhead, and took up our patrol station, it seemed to be an orderly, even easy, invasion – this being observed from 10,000ft. Little did we realise what an awful battle was taking place down there.

In 'Johnnie' Johnson's No. 144 Wing, No. 442 Squadron's activities during D-Day mirrored those of many other units. The pilots were woken at 3.15am and the squadron mounted its first patrol at 6.30am. When the last aircraft touched down at 10pm, No. 442 Squadron had flown 94 hours during four patrols. Each had been led by the CO, Dal Russel, the diary noting that pilots had witnessed 'scenes that were indelibly impressed on their memories – the Channel covered with shipping, fighting on the beaches, gliders landing and battles between Allied and enemy tanks'.

While there was initially little sign of the Luftwaffe, at about 3.45pm the RNZAF's No. 485 Squadron spotted some Ju 88s. These were not bombers, however, but Ju 88C long-range fighters that had been despatched from Brittany. With No. 222 Squadron flying as top

ABOVE Pilots from No. 485 (New Zealand) Squadron relax outside their tent at Selsey just before D-Day. Standing on the left is six-victory ace Flight Lieutenant Owen Hardy and seated, smoking his pipe, is the CO, Squadron Leader John Niven, who also had a number of aerial victories to his name. (RNZAF)

cover, No. 485 Squadron went down after the enemy aircraft, as future ace Flight Officer Johnny Houlton described in his autobiography:

In mid-afternoon I led Blue Section during the third patrol of the day. South of *Omaha* beach, below a shallow, broken layer of cumulus, I glimpsed a Ju 88 above cloud, diving away fast to the south. Climbing at full throttle, I saw the enemy aircraft enter a large isolated cloud above the main layer, and when it reappeared on the other side I was closing in rapidly.

I adjusted the gyro gunsight onto the target at 500 yards, with a deflection angle of 45 degrees, positioned the aiming dot on the right hand engine of the enemy aircraft and fired a three-second burst. The engine disintegrated, fire broke out, two crewmen bailed out and the aircraft dived steeply to crash on a roadway, blowing apart on impact. As I turned back towards the beachhead I sighted a second Ju 88 heading south, so I made an almost identical attack, which stopped the right hand engine. The aircraft then went into a steep, jinking dive, with the rear gunner firing at other members of my section who all attacked, until the Ju 88 flattened out and crash-landed at high speed. One of its propellers broke free, spinning and bounding far away across the fields and hedges like a giant Catherine wheel.

Supreme Headquarters nominated the first Ju 88 I had destroyed as the first enemy aircraft to be shot down since the invasion began, putting No. 485 (NZ) Spitfire Squadron at the top of the scoreboard for D-Day.

A few minutes later No. 349 Squadron, a Belgian unit, shot down two more Ju 88s and damaged a further four, one of the latter among the six claims of Flight Lieutenant Gaby Seydel. Sadly, during an earlier patrol by their countrymen of No. 350 Squadron, a Spitfire VB, flown by Belgian ace Flight Lieutenant François Venesoen had suffered a serious glycol leak, Venesoen becoming the first ace lost in a Spitfire after the invasion had commenced.

Spitfire units patrolled into the night, with, among others, No. 234 Squadron escorting Douglas Dakotas and Airspeed Horsas flying reinforcements to the airborne troops as part of Operation *Mallard*. During what became known as the Longest Day, there had been remarkably little reaction from the Luftwaffe, but that was to change during the coming days and weeks.

The Luftwaffe reaction to the invasion began in earnest on 7 June when, during some hectic action over

Normandy, 34 German aircraft were claimed shot down, almost half falling to Spitfires. Number 401 Squadron was over *Gold* beach early, as its diarist recorded: 'At least a dozen Ju 88s suddenly appeared out of cloud, some managing to dive at the beaches, the rest turning as we attacked and attempting to reach cloud. Squadron Leader Cameron called on everyone to pick his own target, and the squadron broke up.'

The pre-eminence of the RCAF Spitfire squadrons during the Northwest Europe campaign was already beginning, although the RAF also joined the party. Among the latter's units was No. 501 Squadron, led over the beachhead at dawn on 8 June by No. 142 Wing CO Wing Commander Johnny Checketts. During the course of this mission the squadron gained its first victory since the invasion, the action being described as follows in the unit history:

The squadron was vectored to the scene of Luftwaffe activity. Changing course, more enemy aircraft were reported on the squadron's flank, so Yellow Section

ABOVE When New Zealander Flight Officer Johnny Houlton of No. 485 Squadron shot down a Ju 88 on the afternoon of 6 June 1944 it was credited to him as the first aerial victory claimed since the start of the D-Day invasion. (J. A. Houlton)

detached itself and spotted six Me 109s below them, heading away from Le Havre. Flt Lt 'Foob' Fairbanks, the piano-playing American, tore into the enemy fighters, sending one down in flames and badly damaging another.

On 9 June the weather intervened, restricting Allied air activity to little more than defensive patrols over the beaches.

As the fighting on the ground intensified there was also an increase in aerial combat. While losses, mainly due to flak, began to mount, so too did air-to-air claims. Indeed, on 10 June alone, Allied (mainly USAAF) fighters claimed 33 German aircraft destroyed. The first RAF claim of the day came at around 7am, when Flight Lieutenant George Varley of No. 222 Squadron claimed the first of his four victories when he hit an Fw 190 over the beachhead and saw its pilot bail out.

Significantly, 10 June also saw Allied fighters using landing strips in the expanding beachhead for the first time, with aircraft being refuelled and rearmed. Squadron Leader Dal Russel and three others from No. 442 Squadron landed at B3 Ste-Croix-sur-Mer, before returning to Ford at 6pm. The next day No. 453 Squadron's CO, Squadron Leader Don Smith, led 12 Spitfires on a sweep over Normandy and landed at an advanced landing ground for an uncomfortable night's stay – a foretaste of what was to come when 2nd Tactical Air Force (TAF) moved to the Continent.

As Allied troops struggled to achieve the breakthrough that was not to come for many more long, bloody weeks, so the air fighting intensified over the wider battle area, leading to a steady rise in claims and casualties. Flying from Detling on 14 June, No. 80 Squadron had a brief fight. Several hours later, over *Omaha* beach, a patrol from No. 611 Squadron spotted 16 Bf 109s in tight formation just below the cloud base. The resulting attack ended with four German fighters claimed as destroyed. One of these was credited to the CO, Squadron Leader

Bill Douglas, as his sixth victory, leading him to remark 'What a party!' upon returning to Harrowbeer.

Preventing the Luftwaffe from attacking the slowly expanding beachhead and the shipping offshore was a vital task for the fighter squadrons, but for most of the tactical units, armed reconnaissance and ground attack predominated through into July. By the end of June several more Spitfire pilots had become aces over the Normandy battlefield. On the 26th Sous-Lieutenant Pierre Clostermann of No. 602 Squadron was scrambled from B11 Longues (the unit had flown in just 24 hours earlier) and sent after enemy fighters seen flying near Caen. As he passed over the river Orne he engaged four Fw 190s and destroyed one of them near Carpiquet airfield to become the latest Free French ace.

The high point of the aerial fighting over Normandy came on 28 June, with 34 enemy aircraft destroyed (26

OPPOSITE A pair of Supermarine Spitfire Mark IXs of No. 443 Squadron (RCAF) take off from Ford, Sussex, for a sortie over Normandy. Both aircraft each carry a 44Imp gal long-range fuel tank under the fuselage to extend the Spitfire's range over the continent. (IWM HU 92139)

of them by the RCAF) in more than a dozen engagements as the Luftwaffe attempted to support a great tank battle raging around Caen. The last action of 28 June involved No. 401 Squadron, which had been strafing vehicles when 12 Fw 190s bounced it out of the sun. In the ensuing dogfight four German fighters were destroyed. One of these was the first success over Normandy for Flight Lieutenant Irving 'Hap' Kennedy, who already had 13 victories to his name from the Mediterranean. He wrote in his autobiography:

A good old-fashioned scrap followed right down to ground level. My new Spit IX was too much for a Focke-Wulf pilot, who stayed around for the scrap. He had a good aircraft, but could not turn with a Spit IX, and when I got on his tail I knew I had him. One short burst and he was in the trees with a great flash of fire.

After bitter resistance and the almost total destruction of the city by bombing and artillery fire, Caen finally fell on 9 July. This allowed British forces to push

deeper into Normandy, although they faced stiff opposition. As the battles on the ground continued to their bloody conclusion, the fighting in the air over Normandy remained intense. Among those involved in the action was No. 602 Squadron's high-scoring CO, South African Squadron Leader Chris Le Roux, who claimed two Fw 190s and a Bf 109 on 15/16 July. However, it is likely that his greatest contribution to Allied success in Normandy may have come on the afternoon of 17 July when he led an armed reconnaissance over enemy territory. At about 4.15pm he shot down a Bf 109 near Flers and, more significantly, he then strafed a staff car that was later assessed to have been carrying Generalfeldmarschall Erwin Rommel. The commander of Army Group B was gravely wounded. Le Roux's day was not yet over, for that evening he shot down his fifth fighter in as many days.

OPPOSITE Men of an RAF Repair and Salvage Unit working on a damaged Supermarine Spitfire Mk IX of No. 403 Squadron, RCAF, at a forward airstrip in Normandy. (IWM CL 186)

July saw the German forces pushed back further and bombers took part in massive attacks to facilitate the breakout of the Allied army. Dawn on 18 July saw a massive attack by more than 4,000 RAF and USAAF bombers to mark the start of Operation *Goodwood*, the breakout assault of the British 2nd Army. Number 441 Squadron claimed two Bf 109 victories that day.

Into August the Germans continued to battle for Normandy, and on 17 August the ground campaign reached its climax when the Allies took Falaise. On the 19th Generalfeldmarschall Model ordered the German withdrawal, but his forces were already in chaos, and as the Germans attempted to escape, the Spitfires took a grim toll in their strafing attacks; the battle of Normandy was over.

AFTER THE BATTLE

By 22 August the German 7th Army was destroyed and the scene was set for a rapid Allied advance into France. As the Allied armies pursued their defeated enemy, so the fighter sweeps spread ahead, encountering

the Luftwaffe as it attempted to provide some sort of cover for the retreating Germans.

On the 23rd, for example, 'Johnnie' Johnson led Nos 421 and 443 Squadrons on a sweep of the Paris area. Near Senlis the Spitfire pilots engaged a large force of Fw 190s and Bf 109s. Keeping No. 421 Squadron as top cover, he led No. 443 in an interception of the enemy fighters. Six of the latter were shot down, including two by Johnson himself. Above them, No. 421 Squadron claimed six more, including one to Flight Lieutenant John Neil to make him an ace. Minutes later he was in turn forced to bail out and was captured. Despite his success, Johnson was impressed by the performance of his opponents during the fight. 'I was attacked by six short-nosed '190s, which possessed an exceptional rate of climb. By turning into each attack I managed to evade most of their fire, only receiving one hit in the starboard

wing root'. Nevertheless, it had been a perfect bounce.

With more landing grounds now available, further 2nd TAF Spitfire units moved into Normandy, including the Free French No. 145 Wing, which made an emotional move into B8 Sommerviue. It was followed shortly thereafter by the Norwegian No. 132 Wing, which was based at B16 Villons les Buissons, and No. 135 Wing at B17 Carpiquet. For many Wings the move across the Channel was the start of an itinerant existence as they attempted to keep up with the advancing front line. For example, on 21 August No. 127 Squadron moved to the Continent, where it flew fighter-bomber missions from various airfields in France, Belgium and Holland through to VE-Day. It achieved a rare success for a dedicated fighter-bomber squadron when, south of Boos, on 25 August (the day Paris was liberated) it fought a trio of Fw 190s, one of which was shot down by the CO, Squadron Leader Frank Bradley, in a Spitfire IX.

The ADGB Spitfires increasingly provided escorts for daylight raids by Bomber Command 'heavies', the

OPPOSITE Squadron Leader Don Smith (standing) and some of his pilots relax outside a French café after moving to France, where he claimed his sixth, and final, victory on 9 July. (RAAF)

latter mainly attacking targets in the Ruhr. Here, flak proved the main threat, which was an indication of how the situation in the air was changing. On 27 August Bomber Command mounted its first major daylight raid on Germany since 1941 with an attack against a synthetic oil refinery near Homberg, on the Ruhr. The heavy escort included Spitfire IXs from No. 1 Squadron, led by Malta ace Squadron Leader Pat Lardner-Burke, the aircraft fitted with unwieldy and unpopular 90Imp gal overload tanks for the 2.5-hour mission.

The day also saw the loss of a significant fighter pilot when, in the early evening while leading No. 317 Squadron on a sweep over the Seine, Squadron Leader Wladek Gnys was hit and force landed. Wounded in the chest, he eventually escaped back to Allied lines but his flying career was over. Over his native Poland on 1 September 1939, he had shot down two Do 17s to claim the very first victories against the Luftwaffe in World War II. Gnys was but one of a growing number of Spitfire pilots who had fallen victim to ground fire as the hammering of retreating German forces continued unabated.

Such was the speed of the German withdrawal that targets were soon beyond the limited range of the Spitfire units, necessitating frequent changes of base that in turn adversely affected the sortie rate. As September began, Rouen and Dieppe were captured, but bad weather constrained aerial operations. The armoured spearheads continued to drive north into Belgium, nevertheless, with Brussels liberated on the 3rd and the vital port at Antwerp a day later. 2nd TAF wings continued to leapfrog to maintain contact and support, despite the constrictions of the weather. For example, on the 6th, Squadron Leader Hugh Trainor's No. 401 Squadron led No. 126 Wing into B56 at Brussels/Evere – it was the first RAF fighter unit to be based on Belgian soil.

OPPOSITE A No. 421 Squadron RCAF Spitfire Mk XVIE undergoing maintenance in the spring of 1945. (Courtesy of Donald Nijboer)

SPITFIRE ACES

A pilot had to achieve five aerial kills to be considered an ace. While not a comprehensive list of Spitfire aces from the war years, the following highlights the stories of some of the best-known aces and their impressive actions.

FLIGHT LIEUTENANT (GROUP CAPTAIN) COLIN FALKLAND GRAY

Born in Christchurch, New Zealand, Colin Falkland

OPPOSITE Squadron Leader L. C. Wade, Officer Commanding No. 145 Squadron RAF, sitting in the cockpit of his Supermarine Spitfire HF Mark VIII at Triolo landing ground, south of San Severo, Italy, shortly before the end of his second tour of operations in the Mediterranean area, where he had become the top-scoring fighter pilot with 22 and 2 shared enemy aircraft destroyed. (IWM CNA 1979)

Gray joined the RAF in 1938. After completing flying training he was posted to No. 54 Squadron in November 1939, on Spitfire Is. Gray first saw action during the Dunkirk evacuation, and his first confirmed victory was a Bf 109 shot down near Gravelines on 25 May 1940. During the intensive air fighting of the next few months he was frequently in action, and on 15 August was awarded the Distinguished Flying Cross (DFC). He heavily criticised Fighter Command's early tactics and the 'vic' formation. Early in September 1940 Gray's unit was withdrawn from action, with his score standing at 16 enemy aircraft destroyed and one probably destroyed.

During 1941 he spent brief periods with Nos 1, 41, 43, 54, 403 and 616 Squadrons, adding only two more victories to his tally, before being sent to a headquarters post as a rest tour. In September 1942 he returned to operations flying with Nos 403 and 616 Squadrons, before taking command of No. 64 Squadron on Spitfire Mk IXs. Gray was then posted to Tunisia and, after a brief spell as a staff officer at headquarters No. 333 Group, took command of No. 81 Squadron then re-equipping with Spitfire Mk IXs. With that unit he added five more victories to his score, and in May 1943 was promoted to wing commander.

He led No. 322 Wing in action during the invasion of Sicily, and the operations that followed. In October 1943 he returned to Britain to complete another tour as a staff officer. In July 1944 he commanded first the Detling Wing then the Lympne Wing for short periods during operations against the V-1 flying bombs.

At the end of the war his score stood at 27 aircraft destroyed (seven while flying the Spitfire Mk IX) and two shared destroyed, six and four shared probably destroyed and 12 damaged, making him the top-scoring New Zealand fighter pilot. After the war he continued to serve in the RAF, attaining the rank of group captain. Gray retired from service in 1961 and died in 1996.

SQUADRON LEADER (GROUP CAPTAIN) ADOLPH GYSBERT 'SAILOR' MALAN

Born in Wellington, South Africa, Adolph Malan joined the RAF in 1936 and was arguably the greatest tactician of Fighter Command, himself moving away from the 'vic' formation and organising his fighters into three sections of four, as well as using his extensive combat experience to change pre-war thinking regarding the distance from which pilots could engage a target.

On completion of his flying training he was posted to No. 74 Squadron, flying Hawker Demons and then Gloster Gauntlets. Early in 1939 the unit converted to Spitfires, and Malan became a flight commander, being promoted to the rank of flight lieutenant. In May 1940 the squadron was heavily involved in the air fighting over Dunkirk, Malan being credited with three enemy aircraft destroyed, two shared destroyed and three damaged, for which he received the DFC.

In the period between the Dunkirk evacuation and the Battle of Britain, Malan occasionally flew night sorties. During one of these, on the night of 18/19 June, he shot down two He 111s (both confirmed by German records). For this feat Malan received a bar to his DFC. In August 1940 he was promoted to squadron leader and assumed command of No. 74 Squadron. His victory

RIGHT South African Squadron Leader 'Sailor' Malan was one of Fighter Command's most influential tacticians in 1940–41. Having enjoyed great success against the Luftwaffe (including destroying nine Bf 109Es during 1940), he set about changing the types of formations used by RAF squadrons in the wake of his combat experiences.

MALAN'S TEN RULES OF AIR FIGHTING

1. Wait until you see the whites of his eyes. Fire short bursts of one or two seconds, and only when your sights are definitely 'ON'.

2. While shooting, think of nothing else, brace the whole of your body, have both hands on the stick, concentrate on your ring sight.

3. Always keep a sharp lookout. 'Keep your finger out!'

4. Height gives You the initiative.

5. Always turn and face the attack.

6. Make your decisions promptly. It is better to act quickly even though your tactics are not the best.

7. Never fly straight and level for more than 30 seconds in the combat area.

8. When diving to attack the enemy, always leave a proportion of your formation above to act as top guard.

9. 'Initiative', 'Aggression', 'Air Discipline' and 'Teamwork' are all words that 'Mean' something in air fighting.

10. Go in quickly – Punch hard – Get out!

tally continued to grow, and by 1 March 1941 it stood at 15 enemy aircraft destroyed, six shared destroyed, two probably destroyed and seven damaged.

By the end of the Battle of Britain Malan had established a sound reputation as an air fighting tactician. The revised tactical formation that he devised was used by most Fighter Command day fighter units in 1941, and his famous *Ten Rules of Air Fighting* were distributed throughout the Command.

Speaking of Malan, ACM Sir Hugh Dowding commented, 'I looked on him as one of the great assets of the Command – a fighter pilot who was not solely concerned with his own score, but as one whose first thoughts were for the efficiency of his squadron and the personal safety of his junior pilots who fought under his command'.

In March 1941 Malan was appointed commander of the Biggin Hill fighter wing, then flying Spitfire Vs. His final score was 27 enemy aircraft destroyed, seven shared destroyed, three probably destroyed and 16 damaged.

After the war Malan left the RAF and returned to his native South Africa, where he was an active campaigner against apartheid. He died in 1963.

BRIAN CARBURY

The RAF's leading Spitfire ace during the Battle of Britain, and one of only two Fighter Command pilots to become an ace in a day during the battle, when he shot down five Bf 109Es on 31 August, Brian Carbury was born in Wellington, New Zealand, on 27 February 1918. A giant of a man at 6ft 4in, he was also a fine sportsman and an excellent marksman. Following brief employment as a shoe salesman in Auckland, he travelled to England in June 1937 and secured a short-service commission in the RAF, after being turned down by the Royal Navy for being too old. Undertaking his flying training at No. 10 Elementary and Reserve Flying Training School (E&RFTS), Carbury was eventually posted to No. 41 Squadron at Catterick in June 1938, where he flew Hawker Fury II biplanes.

His unit converted to Spitfire Is in January 1939, and in October that year he was temporarily reassigned to No. 603 'City of Edinburgh' Squadron at Turnhouse to help with its transition from Gladiators to Spitfires. He was permanently assigned to the auxiliary squadron upon the outbreak of war and saw his first action in December 1939, when he damaged an He 111 near Arbroath. Carbury followed this up with a share in the destruction of a second Heinkel bomber off Aberdeen on 7 March 1940 and a Ju 88 near Montrose on 3 July.

On 28 August No. 603 Squadron was sent south from Scotland to Hornchurch to relieve the Spitfires of battle-weary No. 65 Squadron. In the coming weeks the unit would claim 67 German aircraft destroyed for the loss of 30 Spitfires. Four of its pilots would also claim five or more Bf 109Es destroyed. Carbury emerged as the unit's ace of aces, downing eight BF 109Es during the first week of No. 603 Squadron's operations with No. 11 Group. Five of these came during the course of three sorties on 31 August.

Carbury was awarded a DFC and Bar in September and October 1940, and by year-end his tally stood at 15 and two shared destroyed, two probables and five damaged.

Like many pre-war fighter pilots to survive the Battle of Britain, he was posted as an instructor to Training Command in December 1940, joining No. 58 Operational Training Unit (OTU). Carbury remained an instructor until dismissed from the service in 1944 following a court martial for bouncing cheques that had been written to cover his wife's opulent lifestyle. Carbury's British pilot's licence was suspended in 1948 for ferrying aircraft to Israel (which was not allowed at the time), and he eventually found work as a salesman for a heating firm. Carbury was diagnosed with leukaemia and died on 31 July 1961.

SQUADRON LEADER (WING COMMANDER) ROBERT ROLAND STANFORD TUCK

Born in Catford, London, Robert Stanford Tuck gained a short-service commission in the RAF in 1935.

On completion of his flying training he was posted to No. 65 Squadron, then flying Gloster Gladiators. Early in 1939 the unit converted to Spitfires, but in May 1940 Tuck was posted to No. 92 Squadron as a flight commander, and by the close of the Dunkirk operation on 3 June his score stood at seven enemy aircraft destroyed, one shared destroyed and two damaged. He was one of the first pilots to score five victories while flying the Spitfire, for which he was awarded the DFC later in June.

During July and August his victory total continued to grow. In September he was promoted to the rank of squadron leader and appointed commander of No. 257 Squadron, equipped with Hurricanes. In October he visited No. 92 Squadron and, flying a borrowed Spitfire, gained a further victory. At that time his score while flying the Spitfire stood at 14 enemy aircraft destroyed, two shared destroyed, one probably destroyed, two damaged and one shared damaged.

In December 1941 he was appointed commander of the Biggin Hill Wing, flying Spitfire VBs.

The following month he was shot down over France and taken prisoner – at the time of his capture his score stood at 27 enemy aircraft destroyed, two shared destroyed, six probably destroyed, six damaged and one shared damaged. Robert Tuck remained in the RAF until 1949, when he retired as a wing commander. He died in 1987.

FLIGHT OFFICER (AIR COMMODORE) ALAN CHRISTOPHER DEERE

Born in Auckland, New Zealand, Alan Deere travelled to Britain along with 11 other New Zealanders to join the RAF in 1937. On completion of his flying training he was given the option of flying bombers or fighters – of course he chose the latter and at the end of his training was posted to No. 54 Squadron, flying

RIGHT New Zealander Al Deere was one of many short-service commission officers to join the RAF during its period of rapid expansion in the late 1930s. Like a number of these pre-war recruits from 'the Dominions', he would enjoy great success in the Spitfire in 1940–41.

Gloster Gladiators. Early in 1939 the unit converted to Spitfires. In recalling the move from biplanes to monoplanes, Deere remarked:

> On 6 March 1939, I flew my first Spitfire. The transition from slow biplanes to the faster monoplanes was effected without fuss, and in a matter of weeks we were nearly as competent on Spitfires as we had been on Gladiators. Training on Spitfires followed the same pattern as on Gladiators, except that we did a little more cine-gun work to get practice on the new reflector gunsight with which the aircraft was fitted.

In May 1940 his unit was heavily involved in the air fighting over the Dunkirk evacuation, and by the close of that operation on 3 June his score stood at seven enemy aircraft destroyed and two shared destroyed – for this success he received the DFC.

During July and August Deere's unit was again heavily engaged, and his victory tally continued to grow. At the end of August it stood at 13 destroyed, two shared destroyed, three probably destroyed and one damaged. Soon afterwards he received a bar to his DFC.

Deere then served a rest tour as a fighter controller, and saw no further action until August 1941, when he joined No. 602 Squadron equipped with Spitfire VBs. In the spring of 1943 he took command of the Biggin Hill Wing when it had just been re-equipped with Mk IXs. In his autobiography he wrote:

> I was now all set to renew my acquaintance with the formidable Focke-Wulf, but this time I was better equipped. The Biggin Hill squadrons were using the Spitfire 'IXB' (Merlin 66), a mark of Spitfire markedly superior in performance to the Fw 190 below 27,000ft… Unlike the Spitfire 'IXA' (Merlin 61), with which all other Spitfire IX Wings in the Group were equipped, the IXB's supercharger came in at a lower altitude and the aircraft attained its best performance at 22,000ft, or at roughly the same altitude as the Fw 190. At this height it was approximately 30mph faster, was better in the climb and vastly more manoeuvrable.

At the end of the war his victory score stood at 17 enemy aircraft destroyed, one shared destroyed, two and one shared unconfirmed destroyed, four probably destroyed, seven damaged and one shared damaged. Deere continued in the RAF after the war, and retired with the rank of air commodore in 1967. He died in 1995.

FLIGHT SERGEANT (WING COMMANDER) GEORGE 'GRUMPY' UNWIN

Of all the distinguished names to appear on the official aces lists, arguably the most experienced Spitfire pilot was the unassuming George Cecil Unwin. Born in Yorkshire, George 'Grumpy' Unwin joined the RAF as an Administrative Apprentice in 1929. In 1935 he was selected for pilot training, and the following year he was posted to No. 19 Squadron, flying Gloster Gauntlets, as a sergeant pilot. He was still with the unit in 1938 when it became the first squadron to convert to Spitfires. When it came to flying the Spitfire, Unwin recalled: 'I've never flown anything sweeter'. However, he also recalled the moment that he first went into action against a Bf 109E over Dunkirk:

> We had been keyed up and raring to go throughout the Phoney War, and fellows like Harry Steere [a 19 Squadron colleague] and myself, with four years of experience already behind us, felt confident in our ability to meet any challenge with the Spitfire as our mount. Despite feeling that my chances of success were good once combat was joined, I still remember that I froze solid in my cockpit when the first Bf 109 attacked me.

By May 1940 he was an experienced pilot, and at the end of that month went into action over Dunkirk, where he claimed his first three aerial victories. During the Battle of Britain his score mounted rapidly, and by November he had received the DFM and Bar. Unwin's score stood at 13 destroyed and two shared destroyed, two probably destroyed and one damaged, making him 19 Squadron's leading ace.

In December he was posted away from the unit to an instructors' course, and early in 1941 he received his commission. A succession of non-operational posts followed and his next combat tour, in 1944, was on de Havilland Mosquitos. He did not add to his victory score however. After the war George Unwin remained in the RAF, and retired from the service as a wing commander in 1961.

FLIGHT LIEUTENANT JOHN CHARLES DUNDAS

Born in West Yorkshire, John Dundas joined No. 609 Squadron, Auxiliary Air Force, in 1938. The unit was in the process of converting to Spitfires when war was declared, and by May 1940 he had scored his first victories during operations in support of the Dunkirk evacuation. Throughout the Battle of Britain the unit was heavily engaged and his victory total grew rapidly.

On 9 October, when his score stood at ten enemy aircraft destroyed, four shared destroyed, one probably destroyed, four damaged and one shared damaged, he was awarded the DFC. On 29 November he was involved in a dogfight off the Isle of Wight during which he shot down Major Helmut Wick, the commander of Jagdgeschwader 2 and then top-scoring Luftwaffe pilot, credited with 56 victories. Almost immediately afterwards Dundas was himself shot down by Wick's wingman, Leutnant Rudolf Pflanz. Both pilots were killed. At the time of his death Dundas had been credited with 12 enemy aircraft destroyed, four shared destroyed, two probably destroyed, four damaged and one shared damaged.

PILOT OFFICER GEORGE 'SCREWBALL' BEURLING

Nicknamed 'Screwball', George Beurling was the highest-scoring ace during the siege of Malta. Born to a Swedish father and English mother in Montreal, Canada, on 6 December 1921, George was a complicated man who left a lasting impression on all those that met him, even briefly. In 1930 he took his first flight and eight years later, at the age of 16, went solo at the controls of a Curtiss-Reid Rambler biplane. Leaving high school shortly thereafter, Beurling got a job as a co-pilot with an airfreight company in Gravenhurst, Ontario. He soon grew bored of this, and after seeing a newspaper article describing the handful of American volunteers heading to China to fight the Japanese, he gave in his notice. Unfortunately for Beurling he was arrested for attempting to enter the US illegally.

With Europe now at war Beurling went straight to his local RCAF recruiter. The latter was unprepared for such a large influx of volunteers, and many, including Beurling, were turned away. Unperturbed, he then tried enlisting in the Finnish Air Force so as to help the small Scandinavian country defend itself from Soviet invasion. Beurling was accepted, but his father refused to sign the necessary papers. In May 1940 Beurling worked his way across the Atlantic to join the RAF. Failing to take his birth certificate with him, the young Canadian was turned away yet again. Returning home to find the necessary paperwork, Beurling was soon on his way back to the UK and in September 1940, the RAF finally accepted him into its ranks.

Following a year of training, Beurling was initially posted to the RCAF's No. 403 Squadron. However, a decision that RCAF units should be manned exclusively by RCAF personnel saw Beurling, who was part of the RAF, posted to No. 41 Squadron – both units were equipped with Spitfire VBs. His first victory occurred on 1 May 1942 when he shot down an Fw 190. Expecting to be praised and congratulated for his first kill, Beurling was instead reprimanded for deliberately breaking formation. Considered a lone wolf and unpopular with his superiors, Beurling was soon transferred to No. 249 Squadron on Malta – then dubbed 'the fighter pilot's paradise' – in June 1942.

His phenomenal eyesight stunned those who flew with him, and many felt safe knowing that enemy fighters could never bounce them. Beurling was neither a smoker nor a drinker, and he was never heard to swear – his prime expletive was 'screwball', hence his nickname.

ABOVE In the centre of this group is Wing Commander 'Johnnie' Johnson, who claimed all 41 of his victories flying the Supermarine fighter. From left to right, Squadron Leader Danny Browne (OC No. 421 Squadron), Group Captain W. R. 'Iron Bill' McBrien (CO No. 127 Wing), Wing Commander 'Johnnie' Johnson, Squadron Leader Jim Collier (OC No. 403 Squadron) and Squadron Leader E. P. 'Eep' Wood (previously OC No. 403 Squadron). (P. H.T. Green collection)

The month after he arrived on Malta, the young Canadian claimed 15 enemy aircraft destroyed and six damaged. After his eighth victory he was awarded the Distinguished Flying Medal, followed by a Bar to this at the end of July. At the end of September, with his score standing at 21.333 victories, Beurling (who had reluctantly accepted a commission to pilot officer the previous month) received the DFC. The 'October Blitz' provided Beurling with another target-rich environment. In just five days he shot down eight aircraft, the last three on the 14th. That same day he was shot down while attempting to intercept a large enemy formation. Hit in the right heel by shrapnel, he parachuted into the sea and was soon rescued. Awarded the DSO shortly thereafter, Beurling was sent back to the UK on 31 October and then posted home to Canada (while on temporary loan to the RCAF) on leave in November.

Returning to Britain in 1943, Beurling became an instructor at No. 61 OTU in July. On transferring to the RCAF, he was posted to No. 403 Squadron and claimed another victory on 24 September, flying a Spitfire IX. Later posted to No. 412 Squadron, Beurling would score his final victory on 30 December 1943 for a total of 31 kills, one shared and nine damaged. Beurling retired from the RCAF on 16 October 1944, but, restless in civilian life, he signed up to fly as a volunteer with the new Israeli Air Force. Tasked with ferrying a Noorduyn Norseman across Europe to Israel, as Beurling departed Rome in the aircraft on 20 May 1948 it blew up, killing both him and his co-pilot. Sabotage was suspected but never proven.

GROUP CAPTAIN (AIR VICE-MARSHAL) JAMES EDGAR 'JOHNNIE' JOHNSON

Born in Barrow upon Soar in Leicestershire, Johnson joined the RAF shortly after the outbreak of war. He first went into action with No. 616 Squadron in December 1940 flying Spitfire Mk Is. Early in 1941 the unit re-equipped with Mk IIAs, and a few months later Mk Vs arrived. During fighter sweeps over occupied Europe he gained his first combat experience and achieved his first confirmed victory, a Bf 109E shot down over northern France on 26 June 1941. On several occasions he flew as wingman for Wing Commander Douglas Bader.

In June 1942, when his victory score stood at seven enemy aircraft destroyed and one shared, he was promoted to squadron leader and took command of No. 610 Squadron with Spitfire Mk Vs. In March 1943 he was promoted to wing commander and took command of the Canadian-manned Kenley Wing, equipped with Spitfire Mk IXs. During the next six months he claimed a further 14 victories, plus shares in a further five kills – for this success he was awarded the DSO. In September 1943 Johnson began a 'rest' tour, and was appointed to the Planning Staff at headquarters No. 11 Group.

In March 1944 he returned to the front line and was appointed to command another Canadian-manned Wing, No. 144, which was also equipped with Mk IX Spitfires. He led this unit during the Normandy assault, and on into the critical first weeks of the invasion.

On 6 April 1945 he was promoted to group captain and appointed commander of No. 127 Wing, which was equipped with Spitfire Mk XIVs.

At the end of the war his victory tally stood at 34 enemy aircraft destroyed (27 while flying the Spitfire Mk IX) and seven shared destroyed, plus a further three and two shared probably destroyed, ten and three shared damaged and one shared destroyed on the ground.

'Johnnie' Johnson was the top-scoring Spitfire pilot of the war, and he achieved all of his victories while flying the type. He was also the highest scoring pilot against the Luftwaffe among the Western allies. Significantly, with the exception of a Bf 110 that was shared, all of his aerial victories were against single-engined fighters.

After the war he continued in the RAF and reached the rank of air vice-marshal.

SQUADRON LEADER NEVILLE DUKE

Born in Tunbridge, Kent, Neville Duke joined the

RAF in June 1940. He commenced operations in April 1941 when he was posted to No. 92 Squadron, then flying offensive sweeps with Spitfire Mk Vs over occupied Europe. On several occasions he flew as wingman to Wing Commander 'Sailor' Malan, who then led the Biggin Hill Wing. He scored his first aerial victory on 25 June 1941 when he shot down a Bf 109F off Dunkirk.

In the autumn of 1941 he was posted to the Middle East, where he joined No. 112 Squadron flying Tomahawks and later Kittyhawks. From then on his score built up rapidly, and by the end of February 1942 it stood at a total of eight confirmed and three probable victories. In April 1942 Duke was posted to the Fighter School at El Ballal, Egypt, as an instructor. In the following November he rejoined his old squadron, No. 92, which by then had moved to Tunisia with its Spitfire Mk Vs.

Duke became a flight commander with the unit, his score mounting to the extent that in March 1943 he was awarded the DSO. In June 1943 his second operational tour came to an end and he was promoted to squadron leader and posted to No. 73 OTU at Abu Sueir, in Egypt, as chief flying instructor. In March 1944 he was appointed commander of No. 145 Squadron in Italy, flying Spitfire Mk VIIIs and when that tour came to an end the following September, he was posted back to England.

His score now stood at 26 aircraft destroyed (eight while flying Spitfire Mk VIIIs or IXs) and two shared destroyed, one probably destroyed, six damaged and two shared destroyed on the ground and one shared probably destroyed on the ground. This made Duke the top-scoring RAF pilot in the Mediterranean theatre.

In January 1945 he became a production test pilot with the Hawker Aircraft Company. After completing the test pilots' course at the Empire Test Pilots' School at Cranfield he joined the RAF High Speed Flight in June 1946, before being posted onto the staff of the Aircraft and Armament Experimental Establishment at Boscombe Down early in 1947. In June 1948 he resigned his RAF commission to take up a post as test pilot with Hawker Aircraft Ltd. In 1951 he became chief test pilot, and in this capacity he was responsible for directing the flight test programme for the new Hunter fighter. In 1953, flying a specially modified Hunter, he raised the world air speed record to 727mph.

WING COMMANDER LANCE WADE

Born in Texas, USA, Lance Wade joined the RAF in Canada in December 1940. After completing his flying training he went to the Middle East in September 1941, flying a Hurricane off the aircraft carrier HMS *Ark Royal* to Malta, and continuing on to Egypt the following day by flying boat. Once there, he joined No. 33 Squadron, flying Hurricanes, and gained his first victories on 18 November 1941, when he shot down two Italian Fiat CR.42 fighters.

When his combat tour ended in September 1942 his score stood at 12 enemy aircraft destroyed. He then returned to the USA for a few months, but in January 1943 returned to North Africa and was appointed to No. 145 Squadron as a flight commander. Wade assumed command of the unit just months later upon his promotion to squadron leader. In March the squadron exchanged its Spitfire Mk Vs for Mk IXs, then in the following June re-equipped with Mk VIIIs. Wade remained in command until November 1943, when he was promoted to wing commander and moved to a staff appointment at Headquarters Desert Air Force.

In January 1944, during a routine flight in an Auster, the aircraft went into a spin at low altitude and crashed into the ground, killing the fighter ace. At the time of his death Wade's victory score stood at 22 destroyed (five while flying Spitfire Mk VIIIs or IXs) and two shared destroyed, one probably destroyed and 13 damaged in the air, plus one destroyed and five damaged on the ground. He was the top-scoring American-born pilot to complete the whole of his combat career in the RAF.

SQUADRON LEADER JOHANNES JACOBUS 'CHRIS' LE ROUX

Born in the Transvaal, South Africa, 'Chris' Le Roux joined the RAF in February 1939. His career as a fighter pilot began in February 1941 when he was posted to No. 91 Squadron, flying Spitfire Mk IIs then Vs. His first aerial victory was on 17 August 1941 when he shot down a Bf 109E near Boulogne. His first tour ended in December 1941 and he was posted as an instructor at No. 55 OTU.

Next Le Roux served as a production test pilot with Rolls-Royce Ltd, flying Spitfire Mk Vs modified into Mk IXs through the installation of the Merlin 61 engine. In September 1942 he returned to No. 91 Squadron and Spitfire Mk Vs, where he quickly gained further victories. In January 1943 he was posted to Tunisia to command No. 111 Squadron on Spitfire Mk Vs and remained with the unit until the end of the fighting in North Africa.

After a spell as a fighter controller, Le Roux took command of No. 602 Squadron in July 1944, equipped with Spitfire Mk IXs. On the 17th of that month, during an armed reconnaissance over the Normandy battle area, he strafed a staff car seen moving at speed in the open. With its driver dead at the wheel, the car ran off the road and crashed into a tree. Its passenger was Generalfeldmarschall Erwin Rommel, commander of the German ground forces in Normandy; he suffered a fractured skull and severe concussion, and had to be relieved of his command.

On 29 August 1944 Le Roux took off from Normandy in bad weather to fly to England, but he was never seen again and was posted missing. At this time his victory score stood at 18 aircraft destroyed (six while flying Spitfire Mk IXs), two probably destroyed and eight damaged.

WING COMMANDER DONALD ERNEST KINGABY

Born in Holloway, London, Donald Kingaby joined the RAF in September 1939. His career as a fighter pilot began in June 1940 when, as a sergeant, he was posted to No. 266 Squadron, equipped with Spitfire Mk Is. He served with that unit and then No. 92 Squadron during the Battle of Britain, and by the end of the year his victory score stood at eight aircraft destroyed. Early in 1941 No. 92 Squadron re-equipped with Spitfire Mk Vs and Kingaby's score continued to mount.

In November 1941 he went to No. 58 OTU as an instructor and soon afterwards received his commission. In March 1942 he was posted to No. 111 Squadron, but a month later he moved to No. 64 Squadron as a flight commander. He was with the unit when it received the RAF's first Spitfire Mk IXs and achieved the first victory in this mark when he shot down an Fw 190 off Boulogne on 30 July 1942. In his after-action report he recorded:

> I sighted approximately 12 Fw 190s 2,000ft below us at 12,000ft just off Boulogne proceeding towards the French coast. We dived down on them and I attacked a Fw 190 from astern and below, giving a very short burst, about ½ sec, from 300yds. I was forced to break away as I was crowded out by other Spits. I broke down and right and caught another Fw as he commenced to dive away. At 14,000ft approx I gave a burst of cannon and M/G [machine guns], 400yds range hitting E/A [enemy aircraft] along fuselage. Pieces fell off and E/A continued in straight dive nearly vertical. I followed E/A down to 5,000ft over Boulogne and saw him hit the deck outside the town of Boulogne and explode and burn up.

In August Kingaby was posted to No. 122 Squadron, a move quickly followed by his promotion to squadron leader in November, after which he took command of the unit. In March 1943 he received the DSO, was promoted to wing commander and took command of the Hornchurch Wing. In September 1943 Kingaby moved to a staff post at headquarters Fighter Command, from where he was posted to the Advanced Gunnery School at Catfoss – here he remained until the end of the conflict.

ABOVE Aces abound in this shot of No. 92 Squadron at Biggin Hill in early 1941 – fourth from left is Sergeant R. E. Havercroft and next to him is Flight Lieutenant C. B. F. Kingcome, then Squadron Leader J. A. Kent, Flight Lieutenant J. W. Villa, Pilot Officer C. H. Saunders, Flight Officer R. H. Holland, Flight Officer A. R. Wright and far right, Sergeant D. E. Kingaby.

At the end of the war Kingaby's score stood at 21 enemy aircraft destroyed (five while flying Spitfire Mk IXs) and two shared destroyed, six probably destroyed and 11 damaged. After the war he stayed on in the RAF.

GROUP CAPTAIN WILFRED DUNCAN-SMITH

Born in Madras, India, Duncan-Smith joined the RAF in 1939. He began his career as a fighter pilot in October 1940 when he joined No. 611 Squadron flying Spitfire Mk Is. Early in 1941 he was commissioned and opened his score on 18 June when, flying a Spitfire Mk V, he was credited with the destruction of a Bf 109E. In August he was posted to No. 603 Squadron as a flight commander, but shortly afterwards was taken ill and spent the rest of the year in hospital. After his recovery Duncan-Smith spent a few months with No. 411 Squadron, before being promoted in April 1942 to squadron leader and taking command of No. 64 Squadron – he was still incumbent when the unit became the first in Fighter Command to receive the Spitfire Mk IX.

In August, Duncan-Smith led his squadron in supporting the large-scale attack on Dieppe, and while covering the Allied withdrawal he recalled:

> When leading squadron at 21,000ft, flying south about 5 miles off Dieppe, I saw three Do 217s at about 5–6,000ft below also flying south. I led the squadron down and I attacked the left one of two who were rather close together. I gave a three-sec burst with cannon/machine gun from 250yds, closed to point blank range, from port quarter closing to starboard and saw large pieces fly off the port engine, wing root and cockpit. When I broke away, the port engine had caught fire and flames were coming from the wing root and the cockpit. The aircraft dived almost vertically into cloud about 1,000ft below.

In August 1942 he was promoted to wing commander and led the North Weald Wing in action. Upon completion of the tour Duncan-Smith had a spell as staff officer at headquarters Fighter Command, then in May 1943 he was posted to Malta, where he led the Luqa Wing for a short period, before being sent to North Africa to lead No. 244 Wing of the Desert Air Force. Promoted to group captain in November 1943, he took command of No. 324 Wing operating in the Mediterranean area, and held that post until March 1945.

At the end of the war Duncan-Smith's score stood at 17 aircraft destroyed and two shared, six and two shared probably destroyed and eight damaged. All of his victories were scored on Spitfires, and more than half of them were achieved while flying the Mk IX. After the war he continued in the RAF as a group captain.

FLIGHT LIEUTENANT RICHARD 'DICK' AUDET

No description of Spitfire aces is complete without mention of the short but brilliant career of the French Canadian Richard 'Dick' Audet. He gained his wings in October 1942 and was sent to England, but once there spent most of the next two years flying with second line units, including an army co-operation squadron engaged in towing banner targets for AA gunners. These humdrum tasks allowed him to build up a large number of flying hours, however, and amass considerable experience in aircraft handling.

In September 1944, with the rank of flight lieutenant, he was posted to No. 411 Squadron equipped with Spitfire Mk IXs, and the following month he was appointed flight commander. By 28 December 1944 he had flown 52 operational sorties and although he had made several attacks on ground targets, he was never in the right place at the right time to engage enemy aircraft in the air.

That changed abruptly on 29 December. The Battle of the Bulge was in full swing and the German fighter force was mounting a major effort to cover the take-off of Me 262 jet fighter-bombers from Rheine airfield near Osnabrück, to allow the latter to attack Allied troop positions in the Ardennes area. Soon after midday, No. 411 Squadron's Spitfire Mk IXEs were scrambled from Heesch in Holland and directed to patrol over Rheine at 10,500ft. Suddenly Audet, leading Yellow Section, caught sight of a dozen enemy fighters below, four Bf 109s and eight Fw 190s, flying in line astern. Audet recalled:

I attacked an Me 109, the last aircraft in the formation. At 200yds I opened fire and saw strikes all over the fuselage and wing roots. The '109 quickly burst into flames and was seen to trail black smoke… I now went around in a defensive circle until I spotted an Fw 190. I attacked from 250 yards down to 100 yards and from 30 degrees from line astern. I saw strikes over the cockpit and to the rear of the fuselage. It burst into flames. I saw the pilot slumped in his cockpit… Ahead was a '109 going down in a slight dive. It pulled up sharply into a climb, and the cockpit canopy flew off. I gave a short burst at about 300yds and the aircraft whipped down in a dive. The pilot attempted to bail out, but his chute ripped to shreds. I saw the '109 hit the ground and smash into flaming pieces… I next spotted an Fw 190 being pursued by a Spitfire pursued in turn by an Fw 190. I called this pilot – one of my Yellow Section – to break, and attacked the '109 from the rear. We went down in a steep dive. I opened fire at 250 yards and it burst into flames. I saw it go into the ground and burn…

Several minutes later, while attempting to re-form my section, I spotted an Fw 190 at about 2,000ft. I dived on him and he turned into me from the right. He then flipped around in a left-hand turn, and attempted a head-on attack. I slowed down to wait for him to fly into range. At about 200 yards I gave a short burst. I could not see any strikes but he flicked violently and continued to do so until he crashed.

Audet made good use of his gyro gunsight during the action and his achievement – five enemy fighters shot down in the course of a single sortie – was witnessed by other pilots in his squadron, and confirmed independently by analysis of his combat camera film. Dick Audet received the DFC for his feat and, having gained ace status in a single sortie, went on to demonstrate that it had been no fluke. In the course of January 1945 he added five more aerial victories to his score, including an Me 262. On 3 March Audet was killed when his aircraft was shot down by flak during a strafing attack on a railway siding. At the time of his death, Audet's score stood at ten enemy aircraft destroyed and one shared destroyed, one aircraft damaged and one destroyed on the ground.

APPENDICES

BF 109E-3 AND SPITFIRE IA COMPARISON SPECIFICATIONS

	Bf 109E-3	Spitfire IA
Powerplant	1,175hp DB 601Aa	1,030hp Merlin III
Dimensions		
Span	32ft 4½in	36ft 10in
Length	28ft 4½in	29ft 11in
Height	8ft 2⅓in	12ft 7¾in
Wing area	174.05ft²	242ft²
Weights		
Empty	4,685lb	4,517lb
Loaded	5,875lb	5,844lb
Performance		
Max speed	348mph at 15,000ft	346mph at 15,000ft
Range	410 miles	415 miles
Climb	to 20,000ft in 7.75 min	to 20,000ft in 7.42 min
Service ceiling	34,450ft	30,500ft
Armament	2 x 20mm MG FF 2 x 7.92mm MG 17	8 x .303in Brownings

C.202 AND SPITFIRE VC TROP COMPARISON SPECIFICATIONS

	C.202	**Spitfire VC Trop**
Powerplant	1,175hp DB 601A-1	1,470hp Merlin 45
Dimensions		
Span	34ft 8in	36ft 10in
Length	29ft ½in	29ft 11in
Height	9ft 11½in	12ft 7¾in
Wing area	180.84ft^2	242ft^2
Weights		
Empty	5,545lb	5,100lb
Loaded	6,766lb	6,785lb
Performance		
Max speed	372mph at 18,370ft	354mph at 17,400ft
Range	475 miles	470 miles
Climb	to 19,685ft in 5.55 min	to 20,000ft in 8 min
Service ceiling	37,730ft	36,300ft
Armament	2 x 12.7mm and 2 x 7.7mm Breda-SAFAT machine guns	4 x 20mm Hispano cannon or 2 x 20mm Hispano cannon and 4 x .303in Brownings

LEADING SPITFIRE MK I/II BF 109E ACES 1940–41

	Unit	Bf 109E Claims	Total Victories
Flight Officer Brian Carbury	No. 603 Squadron	15	15 [+2sh]
Pilot Officer Eric Lock	No. 41 Squadron	15	26
Pilot Officer Colin Gray	No. 54 Squadron	12	27 [+2sh]
Flight Officer Pat Hughes	No. 234 Squadron	12	14 [+3sh]
Sergeant William Franklin	No. 65 Squadron	11	13 [+3sh]
Flying Officer Des McMullen	Nos 54 and 222 Squadrons	10.5	17 [+5sh]
Flying Officer John Webster	No. 41 Squadron	9.5	11 [+2sh}
Squadron Leader John Ellis	No. 610 Squadron	9	13 [+1sh]
Squadron Leader Adolph Malan	No. 74 Squadron	9	27 [+7sh]
Flight Sergeant George Unwin	No. 19 Squadron	8.5	13 [+2sh]

LEADING SPITFIRE V C.202 KILLERS OVER MALTA

	Unit(s)	C.202 Claims	Total Victories
George Beurling, RAF	No. 249 Squadron	6 destroyed	31.333
Henry McLeod, RCAF	Nos 603 and 1435 Squadrons	3 destroyed and 2 damaged	21
John Yarra, RAAF	No. 185 Squadron	3 destroyed	12
William Rolls, RAF	No. 126 Squadron	2 destroyed	17.5
Kenneth Evans, RAF	No. 125 Squadron	2 destroyed	5
James Ballantyne, RCAF	Nos 603 and 229 Squadrons	2 destroyed	5
Lawrence Verrall, RNZAF	No. 249 Squadron	2 destroyed	3
Maurice Stephens, RAF	Nos 249 and 229 Squadrons	1.5 destroyed	22
Colin Parkinson, RAAF	Nos 603 and 229 Squadrons	1.333 destroyed and 2 damaged	8.5
Eric Hetherington, RAF	No. 249 Squadron	1.333 destroyed	3.333
William Walton, RAF	No. 1435 Squadron	1 destroyed, 1 probably and 2 damaged	6

	Unit(s)	C.202 Claims	Total Victories
John Plagis, RAF	Nos 249 and 185 Squadrons	1 destroyed and 1 damaged	16
John McElroy, RCAF	No. 249 Squadron	1 destroyed and 1 damaged	11 plus 3 post-war
George Buchanan, RAF	No. 249 Squadron	1 destroyed	6.5
Ian Maclennan, RAF	No. 1435 Squadron	1 destroyed	7
Claude Weaver, RCAF	No. 185 Squadron	1 destroyed	12.5
Patrick Schade, RAF	No. 126 Squadron	1 destroyed	13.5
John Bisley, RAAF	No. 126 Squadron	1 destroyed	6.5
Ripley Jones, RCAF	No. 126 Squadron	1 destroyed	8
Adrian Goldsmith, RAAF	No. 126 Squadron	1 damaged	16.5
Arthur Varey, RAF	No. 126 Squadron	1 damaged	5.5
Eric Woods, RAF	No. 249 Squadron	1 destroyed on the ground, 1 probable and 1 damaged	11

GLOSSARY

ADGB	Air Defence of Great Britain
AFDE	Air Fighting Development Establishment
AOC	Air Officer Commanding
DAF	Desert Air Force
DFC	Distinguished Flying Cross
DFM	Distinguished Flying Medal
DSO	Distinguished Service Order
E&RFTS	Elementary and Reserve Flying Training School
FAA	Fleet Air Arm, the flying branch of the Royal Navy
LF	Low Altitude Fighter
LR	Long range
IFF	Identification Friend or Foe
OC	Officer Commanding
ORB	Operational Record Book
OTU	Operational Training Unit
RAAF	Royal Australian Air Force
RAE	Royal Aircraft Establishment
RAF	Royal Air Force
RAFVR	Royal Air Force Volunteer Reserve
RCAF	Royal Canadian Air Force
RNZAF	Royal New Zealand Air Force
R/T	Radio transmitter
TAF	Tactical Air Force

EARLY FIGHTER TACTICS

As good as the Spitfire was, its employment in the first 18 months of the war was adversely affected by the rigid implementation of unwieldy tactics. In the 1930s the greatest perceived threat was from the bomber, and, given the range of fighters, and the fact that France was an ally, it was assumed that the bombers would be unescorted. However, the weight of fire of RAF fighters attacking independently was deemed insufficient in bringing down bombers flying in tight, massed formations. The RAF's Air Fighting Development Establishment (AFDE) decided that the only way to solve this problem was to mass fighters in close formation, bringing a large number of guns to bear. Pilots in frontline fighter units were well drilled in formation flying, so a series of six basic patterns known as Fighting Area Attacks (FAA) were duly formulated and published in the RAF *Manual of Air Tactics* of 1938. These were at the heart of standard squadron air drills, as Al Deere recalled:

The majority of our training in a pre-war fighter squadron was directed at achieving perfection in formation, with a view to ensuring the success of the flight and the squadron attacks we so assiduously practised. The order to attack was always preceded by the flight commander designating the number of the attack, such as 'Fighting Area Attack No. 5 – Go'. These attacks provided wonderful training for formation drill, but were worthless when related to effective shooting. There was never sufficient time to get one's sights on the target, the business of keeping station being the prime requirement.

The standard RAF fighter formation at the time was the V-shaped 'vic' of three aircraft. A squadron of 12 aircraft would be split into two flights, A and B, and these were in turn made up of two sections of three fighters. When in full-strength Battle Formation, all 12 aircraft would be tightly grouped together in four sections of three fighters. Leading the 'vic' would be

ABOVE Spitfire Is of No. 19 Squadron head away from Fowlmere in 1940 in tight Battle Formation. The rigid adherence to such unwieldy tactics by the RAF saw Spitfire and Hurricane units sustain heavy losses to marauding Bf 109Es during the Battle of Britain.

the squadron CO or senior flight commander, with succeeding 'Vs' following in close line astern. Once bombers had been spotted, the commander would position his formation in behind them and then lead the attack in section after section. Such attacks would have worked well against German bombers had it not been for the presence of agile escort fighters sweeping the skies ahead of them. As RAF

Fighter Command would soon find out to its cost, FAAs were useless against small, nimble formations of high performance fighters such as the Bf 109E. Indeed, upon seeing British fighters flying into combat in tight, neat rows of three, German pilots, who invariably enjoyed a height advantage, quickly dubbed the vics 'Idiotenreihen' (literally 'rows of idiots').

Those pilots that survived their initial encounters with the enemy soon came to realise that a successful combat formation had to be able to manoeuvre whilst maintaining cohesion. Pilots also had to be able to cover each other's blind areas so as to prevent surprise attacks on the formation. Finally, individual members of the formation had to be able to support each other should they come under attack. The 'vic' allowed for none of these things, and fundamentally, in the 'vic', only the leader searched for the enemy, as his two wingmen had to concentrate on remaining in tight formation, leaving them highly susceptible to attack from behind and below.

The futility of these formations, and the FAA, were brought home to the Spitfire squadrons in their first engagements over Dunkirk, and although numerous pilots abandoned FAAs, 'vic' formations would continue well into 1941 until falling out of practice. Indeed, officially, pilots were forbidden from implementing new tactics at unit level. In reality there was no actual time available for Fighter Command to rectify this problem through the issuing of new tactics on the eve of the Battle of Britain, as future ace Pilot Officer Bobby Oxspring explained:

> We knew that there was a lot wrong with our tactics during the Battle of Britain, but it was one hell of a time to alter everything we had practised. We had no time to experiment when we were in combat three or four times a day. Moreover, we were getting fresh pilots straight out of flying schools who were trained, barely, to use the old type of close formation – they simply could not have coped with something radically different.

A number of squadrons that had seen action over Dunkirk began to modify their tactics. Clearly, combat experience and some amount of 'bending of the rules' ensured survival. In an effort to improve the operability of the 'vic', Fighter Command permitted squadrons to widen out the formations, thus allowing pilots to search the skies for the enemy more freely, rather than concentrating on close formation keeping with the lead fighter. These modifications certainly improved the search and mutual support capabilities of Fighter Command's formations, but did nothing to improve their ability to perform tight turns without losing cohesion.

INDEX

References to images are in **bold**.